The **Power** of Choosing Love

How Broken Pieces Can Fit Perfectly Together - by James & Tanya Wheeler

Believing for a Better You

LOVING WELL WITH JESUS

i

Dear friends,
Let us love one another, for love comes from God. Everyone who loves has been born of God and knows God. Whoever does not love does not know God, because God is love. This is how God showed his love among us: He sent his one and only Son into the world that we might live through him.

1 John 4:7-9

*Above all these things put on love, which
is the bond of perfection
Col. 3:14*

PUBLISHED BY TRIBNET PUBLICATIONS
Sacramento, California
www.tribnet.org

The Power of Choosing Love: How Broken Pieces Can Fit Perfectly Together by James and
Tanya Wheeler

First Edition 2021: Printed in the United States of America. © All Rights Reserved. James and
Tanya Wheeler.

Designer for (external/internal) **book cover**, digital resource bundle, and related artwork (for
workbook/manual and book covers) were created by Rose Ward: The Bloom & Reed Co.
(www.bloomandreed.com). ***Original Designs/Artwork Adapted by Tribnet for printing
purposes.** These designs can only be used by the Believing for a Better You Ministry and the
Bloom & Reed Co. www.bloomandreed.com unless explicit permission is given by Rev. James
and Rev. Tanya Wheeler for use.

ISBN 13: 978-1-7375865-1-7

The Team:
James Wheeler, Tanya Wheeler, Rose Ward and Doug Krieger

Editor: Doug Krieger (www.tribnet.org)
Book Cover (Design Concept): James and Tanya Wheeler
Designer for (external/internal) book cover, digital resource bundle, and related artwork was created
by Rose Ward: The Bloom & Reed Co. (www.bloomandreed.com).
Additional Copies:
To order additional copies of this book and/or other resources created by this ministry please
contact James and Tanya Wheeler (see below).

Phone (916) 581-1261
Email: believingforabetteryou@gmail.com
Websites: www.thepowerofchoosinglove.com **or** www.believingforabetteryou.com

Table of Contents

Dedication & Acknowledgements

We would like to dedicate this book to the profound rescuing work of the Holy Spirit. He, Who in eternity past, moved so many mountains and challenges overcoming all our failures and short comings so that we could finally be bound together in perfect harmony. It is truly the power of His love for us that allows us to become what He perfectly designed us to be—conformed to Christ's image.

Acknowledgment

We acknowledge that this book has been made possible because of the Lord and His amazing grace in our lives. We are grateful as a couple in being allowed to share our experiences with the readers with solely one purpose in mind: to glorify the Lord in all that we do.

At William Jessup University Tanya was greatly inspired by Professor Erin Hill, who believed in our work. She also emphasized the importance of a college degree for this part of our journey. We would like to pay our regards to our spiritual mom, Mary, who listened to the Holy Spirit so closely and gave us the message from the Father that we should be His chosen ones, as people who are set apart for the purpose of the Father to accomplish His great will.

Our blessings to Mary, our sister, who spoke the truth to us and gave us heavenly wisdom as she conveyed to us the deeper truths of our Father. So, we are adhering to the Divine plan and applying what we were advised to do by Mary, which includes honoring each other before the Lord.

We thank the Lord from the depths of our hearts. There are so many people to thank for this book that we did not mention; yet you will read *this* and know that all of you contributed to our journey and helped us to become who we are. Many blessings to all of you.

James and Tanya Wheeler,
Ordained Ministers, Marriage
Mentors, Authors, Speakers, Teachers
-sharing in a Global Ministry in
Kenya Africa and Beyond.

Preface

We are the example in this book to show what real love looks like—with practical tips and insights into healthy marriages. We are sharing our message of hope to those in difficult marriages; preparing those who want to marry, and bringing healing to those who were wounded by divorce. *Let these words of life in our conversational-style interview communicate hope and encouragement to you, thereby bringing you closer to Christ, and enabling you to have a "Jesus-Honoring Marriage" in today's society.*

When you finish reading this book, along with our workbook, we trust that the Holy Spirit will have personally transformed you and your marriage. There is no doubt your communication skills, your confidence, your ability to love yourself and one another will increase through this read. Another benefit is the healing the Holy Spirit will bring by capturing your heart, mind, and soul as you begin to realize all the more who you are in Christ Jesus, which is your truest identity.

One of the things we both agree upon is that we wish we had a book like this to read when we were teenagers or young adults. Sincerely, if we had had the experiential knowledge given in this book, it would have spared us many years of grief, agony, and suffering. It would have saved us from many ill-fated relationships. We could have completely avoided those things if we would have had a book just like this.

The more we thought about writing this book, the more it became clear to us—the sudden realization of why we were writing it brought us to tears. As we reflected on our lives, we truly heard the plea of our hearts crying out.

Yes, our hearts cried out because of the choices we made and the decisions we previously took. As for you, those of you who have been blessed with the opportunity to already make amends—we humbly pray you put into practice the very things that we missed out on . . . the things we failed to put into practice.

After being illuminated to these God-given insights, you will be able to pray over these readings—over each word—with a heart-felt and conscientious desire to change and be renewed in your marriage vows to one another.

This is what this book is all about. We both hope and pray that reading what we have written will prove to be a transformative experience for you.

Introduction

If you keep doing what you are doing right now in your marriage—newlyweds or a seasoned couple—are you 100% confident your current strategy in your relationship will keep you from experiencing additional difficulties or insurmountable challenges that could be prevented like divorce or living through a failed marriage? Are you open to growing into a marriage which fully honors Christ in ways that you have not previously considered? Is the current mental anguish almost too much or regret already too high in your heart and mind? *Do you not only crave hope, but long to learn how to have a healthier relationship from an example that you can understand and easily apply to your own personal life—immediately?* One of the benefits of this read is saving you from what could potentially be a large and long-term counseling expense, or even worse, an expensive divorce, costing you financially, emotionally, spiritually, and even ruining your reputation.

We have been preparing to write a book for many years. It's taken decades to get this book written. Tanya was writing about how to have a deeper relationship with Jesus, and James was writing about the truest godly desires of a marital relationship. Now we are combining these viewpoints into one. Through this book, we are trying to unravel the great mystery of two people becoming one in marriage—a scripturally-based marriage in the Lord.

The ultimate truth about marriage is that Jesus lives in the center of the triad between the two of us; mediating between us while also helping us maintain three separate identities. Like the Father, Son, and Holy Spirit. This is what we have experienced. We want to share our experience with everyone.

It all began by having a deep relationship with the Lord Jesus Christ and then having that remarkable first love, His best love shared with each other in our marriage covenant. It is about closeness and oneness with each other as we have with the Lord—that oneness into which we have been called in fellowship with the Father and with His Son, Jesus Christ.

Max Anders wrote, "Marriage is a picture of the relationship that Christians will have with Jesus in glory. God is a picturing God" (pg. 74). We want to reflect Christ's love through our marriage to the people around us.

Tanya: My relationship with God is the foundation of all my relationships. He is the One to Whom I always turn or the One to Whom I run. No matter what people's ideas or assumptions may be, it always goes back to our relationship with God as the ultimate resort because it lasts forever. For me, He is the Savior and a safe harbor. God's love never fails us; it empowers us to choose love.

James: I have spent most of my life looking for approval and acceptance which I never received as a kid. This mindset took me to places and into relationships that were destined to fail before they really started. Being unequally yoked meant that God's fullest blessing was not available; neither would He ever bless sin.

However, I am forever grateful for my journey and in debt to everyone who has helped me get where I am today, united together—equally yoked—with my most amazing wife.

How Broken Pieces Can Fit Perfectly Together

James: One of the most profound and equally mysterious components of a marital relationship has to do with showing godly, yet natural, affection to my wife all day long. Showing godly affection to your wife establishes a platform that you can build on, the solid foundation of the Lord Jesus. He becomes the rock-solid foundation for a Christ-centered marriage. (Ref. Matthew 7:24-27)

It is the husband's responsibility to build this foundation. When the husband has what he needs—which is love for the Lord—he is more likely to give his wife the love she deserves . . . as Christ loves the Church. You see, a husband cannot give something that he doesn't have first for himself. So first, he must align himself with the Lord. He must choose to be filled with the Lord and His love; then the Lord's abilities will follow.

In the flesh, we cannot love as Christ loves. Fleshly love is considered the root of all sorts of lust. God loves us in Spirit by empowering us with all His spiritual gifts. When a husband walks in the fruit of the Spirit, and in those gifts, it allows him to love his wife properly. It is in those choices made by the husband which enable the wife to launch into becoming everything she is supposed to be in the Name of the Lord.

When she experiences godly love from her husband, she returns that love back to him. As a result, when the husband is loved in return, he is driven and inspired to love God more. The husband then transfers the Word of God, and godly love, back to his wife. The husband then knows it empowers her to become all that she should be in Christ. Once again she returns that love to her husband—it becomes this healthy reciprocal relationship in action.

Our marriage verse is found in Colossians 3:14:

"And above all these put on love, which binds everything together in perfect harmony."

Those actions are the starting place on how and why broken pieces can fit perfectly together.

James: Obviously, women were created to be more emotionally driven; whereas a man is more physically driven. When a man loves his wife and the Lord emotionally, he provides a safe harbor for the wife's emotional needs. When her emotional needs are satisfied, she responds to her husband's emotions. This mutual exchange leads them to be physically fulfilled with each other.

One of the greatest desires of a man is to be physically loved. However, to be emotionally loved by his wife, allows her husband to feel complete. Does that sound like Scripture? Well, yes, because that is the way the Lord designed oneness. The oneness that exists between husband and wife is, in many ways, a great mystery. But here is a bit of an insight into the oneness of the Lord that exists between the Father and the Son. In a sense that even though they are one, they are very much two separate entities—aka "divine distinction." So, as far as the great mystery of marriage goes, my wife and I are one, yet we're two distinct yet inseparable individuals.

Part of that oneness, though, comes from the husband who properly loves his wife. Loving your wife both physically and emotionally allows the husband to be loved back, equally. Nevertheless, the husband must first take his responsibility seriously and submit himself to the Lord. He must rely on the Holy Spirit to give him the godly love that he does not have and can only get from the source of all pure and perfect love, the Lord.

When the husband sees his wife becoming content with the love Christ has provided for her through him and has become all that she's supposed to become, then the Lord causes the husband to return to a fervency in prayer, all the more, for his wife. Husband and wife love the Lord together as one, but individually as well.

This can be viewed as a way of worship which allows the wife to come back to the husband for even more, because she has been loved properly with emotion and physical expression. This exchange is only a representation of the change that has taken place in the Spirit. So, this great mystery of oneness, in marriage, is really about what the Lord is sharing with us.

Tanya: Honey, it is a dream come true—what you just said is exactly what I have always prayed and wanted as a woman. To have a husband who loves me like Christ loves the Church. Without loving Christ, you cannot love me properly. You cannot give me that purity and love, or the intimacy that I so desire. I have learned through you that dreams do come true. It is noteworthy how my husband sent me a text of a note from Panda Express saying, "HAPPILY EVER AFTER DOES EXIST." That is true when Jesus is in the center of the marriage like ours. It is a 3 in 1 situation.

Choosing love is like learning to choose to forgive. Yes, we are making a choice every day—sometimes in our thoughts and sometimes in real-time. Talking about love and choices—we, my husband and I, made a choice too in the forming of our marriage. This in a way is a reflection of Jesus' unconditional love for us.

My ex-husband was abusive and hurtful, but James has not been anything like him. He has genuinely loved and continues to love me unconditionally, just as Jesus loves me; the difference is like night and day. James and I want to share our story of healing, hope, and restoration with our readers. We want to help, give hope, and encourage couples, singles, single moms and dads, remarried individuals and those wounded from divorce. We have mentored numerous singles to avoid unhealthy relationships. We have mentored couples which has resulted in their marriages being saved. We have seen big changes taking place in their lives, all for the glory of God. We will share our experience as an example of all that the Lord has taught us with you in a conversational style with instruction and practical ways to help you understand how to get to the next step, all based upon the Bible. Many Blessings.

Our Prayer for All of you . . .

Father, we pray in the Name of Jesus that Your Word of Truth, and the ministry of the Holy Spirit, brings the necessary healing to the hearts and minds of all those who are married, single, or wounded from divorce who are reading this right now—that they would come closer to You, Lord. Let them experience Your unconditional love and Your redemptive power to help them realize their truest identity of who they are in Jesus Christ. **Fully chosen and accepted in the Beloved**.

We thank you God for the work that You will do in our readers' hearts and minds to transform them into the image of You, Jesus Christ. We pray that all couples learn to love one another the way You designed it, and that each husband will take the lead by loving their wife as Christ loves the Church. Amen.

Our Story

Tanya: As a single mom, I was broken and tired; I was done. I was hurt so deeply that I had given up on life. I remember coming home only to lie down and crying my heart out because overwhelming loneliness had crept in and made a home for itself. My shoulders were tired of carrying the burden of all these responsibilities alone. There was too much stress and so little, if any, support to help me deal with life.

Not only was I a single mom working full time—I was also taking care of my two teenagers who were in a difficult stage of their lives, and at the same time I was going to college. I could not do it anymore. I was at the breaking point. I knew somewhere inside I would go to the hospital with a heart attack, or perhaps a nervous breakdown from the incessant stress in my life.

I could sense something bad would happen to me if things did not change soon. I called out to God to send me help, and He heard my cries for help and answered my prayers. He provided me with the life and love that I longed for. I went through a phase of deep healing—problems that have taken me many years to resolve. It was a long and tiresome process. A lot of people would stay in denial. They would move on with many underlying illnesses—unresolved which can result in serious illness.

I remember as I truly forgave my ex-husband and all other people, it was precisely that moment when the Lord brought me this man of God, James. The man that I had been waiting for, praying, and preparing for so long. James is that treasure that I saw in a vision; I just did not know it was this wonderful man. I have always desired and wanted a husband to love and cherish me as Christ loved the Church. I remember asking the Lord to allow me to experience real unconditional love, with a real man of God before I die.

Now I can say that I have experienced Jesus Christ's real unconditional love, His kindness, gentleness, and tenderness. That has given me hope to believe again, and a God-given desire to experience this hope with my husband. I knew what this hope was all about.

This love was all I had that helped me get through terrible experiences. It is a truly fulfilling experience that I pray a lot of people get to experience. Yes, that they also get to understand the real, true love of Jesus Christ in their hearts.

This is where the new journey has begun in God's perfect timing. *Perseverance and obedience are what it took for me to come to this place to meet my husband, James.*

James: As a single man, I remember waking up in the household where I had rented a room from a couple. Time and time again, I would just ask the Lord for what my next step should be. I was newly divorced from a woman who abused me in silence. I was challenged to come face to face with my inner self through an ugly divorce.

I had lost my business partner of many years to the side effects of breast cancer treatment. I was so emotionally spent. I was physically in the best shape of my life, but I was failing to invest in my own peace. So, I decided to move out to another state. I had had enough of all the heartache from the abuse, neglect, and being unequally yoked. My heart was broken as I wondered how a man as kind as myself was seemingly always getting hurt by women.

Why did I continually choose so poorly when it came to relationships? I was ashamed of myself. While out of state, I began to rediscover myself and who I truly am in Christ. I began my journey of finding God on the mountaintop, where later, I was able to take my wife Tanya. I began to meet one of the pastors of Westside church every week for a few months and I got myself a good psychologist.

One of the many things that I discovered is that I was desperate to get approval and acceptance from someone—an unconditional love that I never received from my dad. *I was trying to fill that void in my heart with relationships that did not glorify God.* I found out and already knew that God wanted to fill in that void in my heart and heal my heart of the wounds that my dad inflicted upon me.

At first, I was struggling to believe that I could finally become someone, somebody who mattered because I had failed so many times. I felt so condemned. I had to break the habit of beating up myself. In my head, it was as if the laughter of many family and friends played nonstop; I believed those lies in my head because I was convinced they were true. There came a point when I knew that my time out of state was coming to an end. I had put things into storage.

I called my mom and told her that I felt like it was time to come back to California. She told me that I could just stay in her spare room for some time and contemplate what the next step was. I had some of my things in storage. I remember when the Lord told me to go and pack my things because it was time to leave the next morning. I told God it was raining outside—this could readily delay my moving plans. He told me to go and pack my things anyway; so I stopped arguing with God and went.

When I got to the storage place, it stopped raining until I was done. When I began to drive off the storage unit property, it started raining just as I left. Seems like God really was in control of all things. Then it happened. I was in the middle of nowhere, and I was getting a call on Facebook messenger. I thought, "How is this possible, I'm nowhere near any signal or Wi-Fi" . . ..

It was my friend who used to go to the same church as I did in the past. I remembered the words that I had spoken before the Lord, "If I ever have the honor and privilege of seeing her again, I won't miss it next time."

So, I answered the call. It was Tanya, hallelujah! She had met with me in the past with questions on finances while we were building a friendship. Once again, she had some questions related to finances and how to properly prepare for her financial future. I told her, "Let's meet at Chili's Restaurant." The meeting was set. When we saw each other, we both knew that God had a plan, and we both immediately had that feeling of just belonging to each other.

Finally, I made a move because I felt like God was moving and this was His plan for me, for us. When I was not seeking a woman, God sent me a wife. This woman was perfectly crafted just for me. She became my best friend who loved me unconditionally and accepted me for who I am. My heart was finally contented, fully at peace, like I was finally home.

So here we are. We are so excited about this new adventure. All the new things that God has in store for us, and how God will shine through our story—our love story. How God put us together. After the story, we will share an instructional workbook with couples. Let your adventure begin with us.

We pray that our redemptive love story in this book will give you hope and that you realize all the more how much you are loved by the One and only true living God. Blessings.

Our marriage is a testimony of God's Redemptive Power, of His love and a living example, a picture, and a glimpse of the relationship between Father God and His Son Jesus and to His Church, All Glory to God.

SECTION ONE: LOVE

"The greatest of these is LOVE

1 Cor. 13

Husbands, love your wives, just as Christ loved the church and gave himself up for her . . . .

Eph. 5:25

4

Chapter 1:
What is True Love?

What is love? It is the willingness to base our marriage upon our love for Jesus Christ. Choose anything else like fear, fame, etc., and you will find out that it will not be able to hold up against the issues life throws at you—and there are a lot of "issues." So, how do you build your marriage on your love for Jesus Christ?

One of the most important practices is to spend time with the Lord and let Him build the foundation and structures of your life (Psalms 127:1). Who better to build our lives than the Lord Himself? That is how we get success. We all know everybody desires success especially in relationships.

We want to be successful in every area of our lives, whether it is personal, social, work or more. Now we know how to make it happen. We have to constantly keep ourselves in check and ask ourselves. Are we allowing the Lord to build our "Home," our marriage, or are we trying to do it all based on our own strength?

A strong relationship between spouses reflects the love of God to all the people around us. We are the physical example of what a marriage that is committed to the Lordship of Jesus Christ should look like. It is almost as if Jesus Christ Himself was present here. Our marriage should be the truest example of God's love for all humanity to see.

Our marriage is the truest example of God's love for all humanity to see.

Tanya: Honey, what is true love?

5

James: The secret of life is to learn how to love each other. Love is not just a feeling. It is a commitment, an action, a responsible choice that we make daily. ABC in marriage stands for *Always Be Committed*. It means that you intentionally choose to treat each other wisely and to accept one another for who you are. It means that you constantly show your love and respect for each other. It involves being intentional in your pursuit of quality time with the Lord—the source of perfect and pure love. True love consists of resembling the very nature and character of the Lord (1 John chapter 4*). Love is a choice to give of yourself and dying to self for the better of another person.*

Tanya: What actions do I take to love myself?

James: There was a time when I would look in the mirror, and before I really knew the Lord, I would always find my deficiencies and all my shortcomings. Also, I judged myself harshly. As much as I wanted to feel good about myself, I could not because the only standard I was using was the standard of my own understanding. When I surrendered my life to the Lord, and I understood His standards, that is when my life changed.

I understood that God's standard is "unconditional love." This is the love that accepts us exactly for who we are. I am the creation of God. He created me to be exactly who I am. He has made me perfect in His sight. Once I focused on His perfection for me, I was able to look in the mirror and see His workmanship in my life, not my shortcomings or defects.

Although I know I am not a perfect looking man, I can see His loving touch all over my face. Because he loves me perfectly for who I am—because I am exactly how He made me. As James Ronald Wheeler, it is impossible for me to be anyone else; God uniquely created me.

Tanya: Amen. That is so true because this is the cycle of love. First, we receive the unconditional love from the Lord by having a salvation experience with Him which puts us in proper relationship with Him. Then we give it back to Him and say, "Thank You God for creating me in your image." This should be our response to His message of pure love. Then we have the capacity to love ourselves for who we are because we accept ourselves just as He accepts us. Then we can give godly love to others; then we can actually receive that love back with the capacity to properly understand love. Then we move on to give it to the community and to others. That is precisely what the Lord showed us. It is a "full circle" wherein we receive God's Love—then we are able to love God in return—then to love ourselves as He does—and then to love others as we are loved by God.

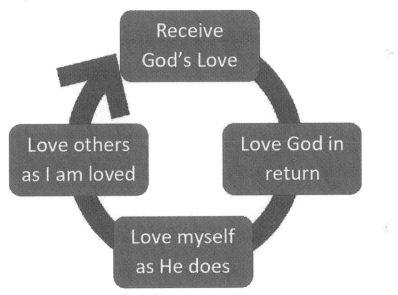

Before the Lord heals your heart and shows you how valuable you are, you need to receive love from God first. Otherwise, you cannot receive other people's love before that. You do not know how to receive love until you understand the perfect, unconditional love of God. This love will allow you to love yourself and others the way Christ does without any conditions. You will simply love others. This is what will enable others to return and love you in a godly way.

This is, as well, the inner healing which starts first from the heart. Then it goes from the inside to the outside, and that is when the beauty comes out so deeply. Thank you, Lord. Amen.

Life-altering Moments

Here, I want to share some of the most important moments in my life. These are the times which led me into the love of God. Before I found Jesus, I believed that I had to earn love. I believed that I had to do some kind of a great work to please God, to hear Him, and to be allowed into His heavenly presence.

I distinctly remember when I was 18 years of age, I felt this great longing to know the truth and to find out what love is. I wanted someone to love me, but what was this love? How would I know if someone is loving me or not? What I was really looking for were ways to know God and to directly hear from Him.

Although my life was good in a physical sense, I knew there was something missing. There was a void that was constantly there and no matter what I did, I could not fill it. One day I just went into my room, got down on my knees, and started praying. I saw myself, as a little blonde girl, running to God and Jesus picking me up in His arms. That is when I knew He loved me. Heavenly Father was always with me and always loved me.

Still, I did not know what a real relationship with God looked like. Ten years elapsed . . . then I had another moment. I remember it so clearly. It was in March of 2008. I was in Florida. I had a lot of anger in me at the time. So much so that my veins throbbed with it. I kept praying and praying—I felt I had to somehow pray through for hours before I could feel the presence of God.

At times I felt like it was all for nothing. I was depressed, empty, frustrated with God for not listening to me. Really, it virtually drove me to the brink of suicide. I remember picking up the Bible and reading Proverbs 3:7, *"Be not wise in your own eyes; fear the Lord and turn away from evil."*

I also remember turning on the TV and watching Joyce Meyer. She was talking about salvation and asking us to follow her in a prayer. I repeated the prayer and accepted Jesus Christ as my Lord and Savior. It was then I felt like I was saved—my life was going to change. I finally knew what the love and grace of God was.

Ever since that time, I have longed for a closer relationship with God. My eyes had been opened. I finally knew what the love of God was. Now, I wanted something more. My journey into a relationship with God moved on at a steady pace—I kept going deeper and deeper. I longed to experience His love every day.

His voice would say, "I love you my daughter. I am with you. I hear you and I care about you." His voice was always gentle, kind, and loving. It felt like a deep embrace. It was like Someone was walking beside me. I never felt alone after that initial salvation experience.

Tanya: Honey what are the steps for people to know and experience the love of God?

James: The very first step in knowing the love of God is to pray and ask Him to come into your life as your Lord and Savior—Tanya, that's what you did. Ask yourself, "Have I truly asked Jesus into my heart?" If you have not, get down on your knees and cry out to the Lord:

"Lord Jesus! Thank You for Your love. Thank You for dying for my sins. You are the only one Who can forgive me. Without Your forgiveness, I will be eternally lost. Dear Jesus! I humbly ask that You come into my heart, forgive me. I commit my life to You. Be my Lord and Savior. Thank You Jesus! Amen."

Do this dear friend and you will know that you have been saved by His everlasting love. This is the best thing that could ever happen to you. We are so happy that we get to celebrate this day with you—we welcome you into His eternal family!

Tanya: What does true love look like? I was praying to God and asking Him, "Lord what am I missing?" God said, "Love!" I asked Him, "Lord, how do I love, help me?" That is when I read 1 Corinthians 13: 4-8:

> *"Love is patient, love is kind. It does not envious; it does not boast, it is not proud. It does not dishonor others, it is not self-seeking, it is not easily angered, it keeps no record of wrongs. Love does not delight in evil but rejoices with the truth. It always protects, always trusts, always hopes, always perseveres. Love never fails."*

Love is patient. That is like the first thing that comes out. Love is not prideful. God said, "I am love, I am patient, kind, protective, trustworthy." "Lord, I declare that I am always patient, kind, and gentle—this is who I am in You." So, I see that in God's love, and how we are supposed to live by His love. Love tells us everything about how we're supposed to live. Because God is love, and I can love too. The Holy Spirit lives inside of me to help me. I am to protect my marriage and trust God and my husband too.

What is love?

Tanya: Love is patient and kind, and all things that are good. It is the four circles of life. First, it is God showing us His unconditional love, and we are receiving and experiencing that from Him into our hearts. Second, we return that love back to Him in true honor of every aspect from our heart.

Third, we choose to love ourselves exactly for who we are and how we are created with all our weaknesses, flaws, failures, appearance, talents, and strengths. Finally, and fourthly, would be loving other people—all of them without any judgment or criticism.

"Love the Lord your God with all your heart and with all your soul and with all your mind and with all your strength. Love your neighbor as yourself. There is no commandment greater than these." (Mark 12: 30-31)

This should be our focus: How to love more.

In John 15:13 we read: *"No one has greater love nor (stronger commitment) than to lay down his own life for his friends."* This is like my husband does many times for me by putting me first. He shows me selfless love and honor.

Joyce Meyer wrote:

"The love of God is meant to be a powerful force in our lives, one that will take us through even the most difficult trials into victory."

God's love has brought me through all the deep waters of my life. His love never failed me. It is always constant and never changes. We can go to the Father's throne of grace and abide in His love. This is the safest place to be.

Love is worth fighting for, because it is what every human needs. It overcomes and conquers everything which comes against us. It is our mission to find it and choose it for ourselves. That is how we find true happiness and satisfaction.

Here we are writing the first chapter of our first book. Then I (Tanya) receive a text from a friend. I opened the text to find a beautiful red rose. The rose opened up and the message revealed said: *"You're a beautiful rose. Have a beautiful, blessed day!"*

Wow! The timing was perfect. That is how much God loves me. He sends me these little messages throughout the day to show me that He loves me. I replied to the message by telling my friend how I was writing a book with James about the love of God.

She texted back, "That's so amazing! God's love is such a difficult concept to understand and explain. It is something so much more than a Mother's love for her child. I am so proud of you. I pray that God uses your books to touch people with His presence." This is God's love.

How to live out life in love?

Tanya: Living to love includes every area of our lives. It deals with how we live daily and how we communicate with each other. Love is a choice—a choice that we make every day, even moment by moment. Because if we do not live by it, we risk falling prey to sin. When we choose to love, God helps us to really love each other by obeying His Word. That is what this whole book is about. It is about choosing love. Love is an action; it's how we live.

In 1 John 4:19 it says: *"We love because He first loved us."* It is so deep. In his book, *Loving Solutions,* Gary Chapman says:

> "The final principle for reality living declares love to be the most powerful weapon for good, and that especially applies in marriage. The problem for many husbands and wives is that we have appropriate behavior. It affects the emotions, but it is not itself an emotion. Love is the attitude that says. 'I choose to look out for your interests. How may I help you?' Then love is expressed in behavior" (page. 49).

Love is an action, not an emotion. Many couples think they are in love because of feelings they are experiencing. Love cannot be separated from action—behavior that demonstrates respect and honor and preferring one another.

Tanya: Honey! You have been so strong throughout your cancer treatment. Your attitude is so positive. You trust God's will in everything. I could have been the one with cancer, but you took my place. If it had been I in your place, I would not have been able to go through with it like you have. I would not have had the attitude that you have.

I am so happy that I have a life with you. A life where I can experience true love from you—from Jesus. I have learned to love you and accept you as you are. It has been such an amazing journey with you.

I still remember our vows when I was asked:

"Tatyana! Do you take James to be your lawfully wedded husband? To love and to hold, from this day forward? Do you promise to love him and comfort him, to honor him and keep him, in sickness and in health, in prosperity and adversity, and forsake all others, to be faithful to him?"

I said, "I do!" God told me to love you as you are. This is what real, unconditional love is all about.

James: Sweetie! We are partners in everything. One of the greatest blessings to me is that we love and accept one another unconditionally, which is true godly love. I'm so thankful that I can call you my wife, best friend, co-parent, partner in ministry; my buddy to go and have fun with at the beach or the woods; my business partner; and my partner for life in all things. Yes, we're a team and co-laborers for the Lord!

Those marriage vows are always circulating in my head like a song of love that God sings over me, over us. It is a song of His healing love in both of our lives, and as one in Christ.

This is what real love is. We experience it every single day of our lives. It is so deep that we met each other or even got closer to each other in the hardest of times, during our worst of times. This was our nadir—the worst version of who we are. Amazing, we haven't even seen each other at our best!

Can you imagine what God is going to do with our brokenness—our broken pieces? How He is putting us together and raising us up together? It's so powerful. It is like, WOW!

Tanya: I absolutely love you, my husband, for the person you are. You love me for me with all my imperfections. Many of the wrongs, different issues, in my cultural background were exposed. **But I understood it was/is so important to love a person for who they really are in their heart, as a person. That was and is key.**

Once I was forgiven and forgave others . . . once I had let go of my past . . . then I desired true friendship. Finally, I was in a place where I wanted to share my life with someone else. Someone who would love me like Christ loved the Church. I found that first with Christ, and then with you, James.

When you came into my life, you were exactly what I wanted. You became the exact representation of Christ's love for me. Someone who would show me physical love . . . just as I have spiritually experienced it. You took me as your bride; now our relationship is a beautiful representation of God's love.

In Romans 8:39 I see that nothing will be able to separate us from His love. Also, Isaiah 54:5 tells me that Jesus is my husband. He is my first love and my second love is my James.

James: I agree! One of the deepest truths that we can pass on is when we choose to love; it binds us together in perfect harmony. What love do you choose? It is godly love. The love that is gentle, patient, kind, considerate, and forgiving. This love holds no wrongs against each other; so we can see each other for who we are in Christ Jesus. When you consider what I'm saying, well, it's simply walking in Christ's character—this is more than enough.

So, when we put on love (Col. 3:14) which is Christ's character, it demonstrates to us what God says: He is love—it is just the manifestation of His perfect harmony. The harmony in such relationship is perfect because it includes God. Love without God has no perfection; it has no perfect harmony. It is only human effort.

Whenever we choose love, it is like turning on the light. When you turn on the light, the darkness cannot exist anymore. So, it is all about choosing. Even if you feel the other person is not deserving, you can choose to turn on the light and remove all darkness. When you do it God's way, by turning on the light, it gets rid of the enemy. It allows you to come back together to bind in perfect harmony. It is all based upon God's love Who always loves.

This is, hopefully, just a helpful, little nugget of a secret of how my wife and I maintain a great marriage, and how we continue to grow in it. Because we choose to love at every occasion. **We choose love, which gives no place to the enemy.** That allows us—by walking in the Light (His Light)—to be bound together in perfect harmony. This way, we get rid of all the darkness.

When you put on love, a part of love is godly forgiveness. True forgiveness allows us to stay in a place of humility. Christ was humble and gentle at heart. When you choose to walk in the humility and gentleness of Christ, that in and of itself produces the fruit of the character of God in you. It allows you to make those decisions to love as Christ loves—it binds us together in perfect harmony. Stay tuned for more blessings. Amen.

Tanya: Honey, can we talk about how you demonstrate this love to me? First, however, I want to explain it myself!

15

You demonstrate this love to me in words and actions. By speaking kind, loving words like, "I love you" or "You are awesome." I love the tone of your voice when you talk to me, tenderly and gently. When you show me this kind of love by hugging and embracing me daily, emotionally and physically connecting, helping me out with chores, texting me loving words with hearts—that speaks your mind to me.

These are examples, James, of the many texts that you regularly send me:

"Sweetie, I am so thankful to the Lord for you 🙏🌸🌷🍫😊😄 I love who you are becoming in the Lord, how you are developing your identity in Christ Jesus. I love and appreciate your affection towards me as I walk through this season and overcome these things. I am sorry that my super dry mouth doesn't allow me to kiss you the way I want to kiss you.

"You're truly patient my love 🖤😊 I love our time together 🖤😊🤝 It's just awesome to go through life together . . . launch our book and ministry and all that the Lord has planned for us. I love just feeling you, cuddling up with you, and just being with you 🖤😊🌷🍫 😊😊 please come and snuggle with me my love 🖤😊😄🖤😄😊🍫."

I pray that your husband will text you like that.

I know that my husband's fight against cancer has really affected both of us. I am thankful that I still get to be with him, hug him, rejoice with him, wake up every morning next to him. I am so thankful he is alive. I know that there is a lot of work to be done. We so desire to serve the Lord—neither one of us can be sick anymore. That is why I accept wholeness and healing.

Looking at our life together, I am so thankful that I fell in love with the man of my dreams—someone who truly loves me and cares for me—someone who knows what I am inside and loves me for it—someone who doesn't go for my outward looks like most men.

He looks deep inside me and loves me for me, as a beautiful woman of God. I love how we dance together to worship music; how we read the Bible together—talk, pray, watch movies, hug each other, and just peacefully sit together.

Honey, you are who you are—genuine, truthful, honest, opening your heart to me to let me hear what is inside your thoughts, etc. you are vulnerable with me, and selfless by choosing to be intentional and putting me first. That is loving me the right way.

This proves to me that you are a real man who unconditionally loves me. It is not about a man's looks or muscular prowess. Men can think in their own selfish way, but it is being as Christ—gentle and kind. That is really what a real woman wants and desires to experience.

For me, love is proven true in our hardest moments of life. James, when you had to go through cancer treatments, we learned to overcome our fears with God's grace. We had to love each other even more. We celebrated every little victory— like every bite of food that you could eat.

I love the fact I now understand how the human body is so fragile; how our strength is from the Lord and not from ourselves. I can only depend on the Lord to give us strength, wisdom, and direction.

It is such an honor and a beautiful thing to take care of you with joy, Honey! To give you water when you are so thirsty and have dry mouth from your treatments. You have always taken care of me in my hardest of times—you would listen to my cries, my hurt, my pain. You love to cook, clean, and take care of our home and our children. Thank you so much.

Even in the good times I can come and share with you about what happened in the meeting group and how people love me and accept me. It is just so beautiful to share everything with you, my love. Thank you for always listening, caring, and trying to understand me. So, Honey, what is love? And how should we live by and model it? What are the nuggets that you can share?

James: I think, for me, love is allowing the Kingdom of God to flow out of me; just what is love? Love begins with modeling. What was the role modeled by Jesus? Anyone can say there is no greater love than to lay your life down for a brother. I think, wow, that's kind of weird. What he is talking about is sacrificial love; it helps you set aside your own stuff for the benefit of someone else. You pay the price and the consequences.

I think real, true, pure, godly love is being willing to set aside your own will and your own desires. It is for the benefit of others, and especially for your wife. Now, Jesus says through Paul, "*Husbands, love your wives, as Christ loves the church.* (Eph. 5:25) What does that mean? That means, as Paul says, I am to "wash" my wife daily in the Word of God (Eph. 5:25-27). My best interpretation is that love lets the Father—the love of the Father—flow through me, and demonstrating Christ's type of love to my wife in my actions and words.

Part of this washing with the Word is my conversation time with you. To wash you in the Word is intentionally communicating with you. Meaning, I must be willing to open my heart and become vulnerable, to share my real heart and thoughts with you. It has to do with just enjoying my conversational time with you; to talk as best friends would, and certainly how a husband and wife should.

It is listening carefully to what you are saying and clarifying what you say, so we don't allow any misunderstanding to come between us. It also proves to you that I value you by opening my heart and mind to you. It communicates that I do not want to share those thoughts or those areas of my heart with anyone else—so our deepest intimacy is built up even stronger.

In fact, my words only have value in light of my actions; they prove what my words say. My actions better align with the fruit of the Spirit. If I am not representing those things, I am not actually accurately representing love, which means I am not accurately representing the Kingdom. That is because God says, "I am love." I need to express love myself through the power of the Holy Spirit. So that way, I can love others, and it allows me to be a lovable person.

As a man, this goes against the "world's" philosophy of what a man should do and say. So, as a man who follows Jesus, we need to be mindful that this is part of our transformation. We need to set aside the world's standards and influence on our lives of what a "man" should look, talk and act like. We are called to be transformed into the image of Christ Jesus.

The greatest ministry of Jesus' ministry was to reveal the true love of the Father to us. That means setting aside your own pride, arrogance, ambition, the need to be right, and the need to feel that you are better than others. Just put that aside and walk in a humble life that says:

"I'm so prone to sin and to wrong thinking, because of my carnal nature, that I can become disillusioned by my own mind. I must align my mind with the thoughts of Christ and to think Kingdom thoughts and see things the way that the Father sees them because the Father is the author of love; He is love. Only through Him can you give what you don't naturally have. Our natural state of being, even as a Christian, is that battle of our carnal nature, which doesn't allow us to love perfectly."

So as we put aside, as Paul says, "our carnal nature," to take off the old and to put on the new, it allows us to become a pure form of love because it's the godly love that we get to extend to others and to act out in our own life. This comes through

19

the very nature of God, of being humble, being a servant, being gentle, being kind, not defending your own position, not being proud, not keeping a record of things that were done wrong in the past.

A lot of things go into portraying the image of Christ in our lives. That is why I think Jesus says to die to ourselves, pick up His cross, and follow Him. His cross was His greatest demonstration of love. When we put down our old nature and allow him to resurrect us up in His nature, we become as loving as possible. We will never love perfectly until we are in glory. We are called to be like Him. So that's a few of my thoughts.

Tanya: How do you get there, Honey? Like, it is hard for men to find the time. You know, how do they become the expression of this love you're talking about. What did it take for you to get to that place of expressing His love?

James: It was not me. It was just a work of the Holy Spirit. I would like to say I fully desired to be changed. I really did, but at the same time, I understand the sovereignty of God that says, I am the author and the finisher of your faith. My desires are only there because of the prompting of the Holy Spirit, which is a profound amount of love. The Holy Spirit could simply let me continue to run astray with my own best interpretation of everything. But my desire is just to know God more deeply, not being caught up with my carnal nature—just obeying the desires of my flesh.

One of the greatest things that God had to teach me is what love is. I grew up in a family that did not practice love. They were not loving. Things were done out of anger and fear. As you know, unrighteous anger is of the enemy. So, I realized by the prompting of the Holy Spirit that for me to become more loving, I had to hang out with more loving people. That was kind of an option. Really, I needed to spend more time with not only the One Who is altogether more loving, but Whose

Life was the perfect example of Love, because His very nature and character is love.

After spending time with the Lord daily, one of the thoughts that I've turned into action is this: "I'd rather be in a right relationship with my wife than just being right." The Holy Spirit also made it very clear to me that we do need to be in the right relationship with the Lord and with our wives. This is the love relationship that flows out because too often we as followers of the Lord don't necessarily live in a way that we fully understand how much God truly loves us.

If we really understood how much God genuinely loved us it would change our mindset and our behavior completely. At a minimum it would bring a vast improvement in the way that we see our wives and love our wives because it's from a different starting place, a kingdom mindset.

It's a different point of reference, because now we're looking at our wives through the lens of Jesus, just like the way the Father sees His own Son. It's that pure love that brings the transformation that we all desperately desire. We pray that you may experience the love of Jesus and become one with Him and your spouse.

THEREFORE, what *God* HAS JOINED *together,* let no one *seperate.* Mark 10:9

Chapter 2:
The Two Become One in Christ

The two become one in Christ, Father, and Son. They reflect the oneness of marriage.

We are convinced that if you want to have the best marriage, you must have Jesus Christ as the foundation and center of your marriage. We ought to never lose sight that the Lord has joined us together as one in Christ, in a marriage covenant. *"Therefore, what God has joined together, let no one separate"* (Matt. 19:6). It is a profound mystery how we are one because of the Holy Spirit living inside within our human spirit—"For he that is joined to the Lord is one spirit" (1 Cor. 6:17).

Tanya: Honey, I love and enjoy our moments when we go out for walks and talk together. When we sit and watch the beautiful birds flying around and all the butterflies. We enjoy being in love with each other, just like in the garden of Eden when Adam was with Eve. They were one, in love, and enjoying a beautiful, pure, perfect place. They were in harmony with each other about everything. I like how we talk about the changes we see in nature and our lives; how each season of our life changes daily and weekly. We talk about our plans, children, ministry, business—everything.

We stop and ask the Lord what does He want to speak about to us in those moments . . . what is on His heart? We hear Him speak inside of our hearts because the Holy Spirit lives inside of us and we are one with Him. There are times we hear the same thing. Even yesterday when I was thinking about something, and Honey, you said it to me already when I was

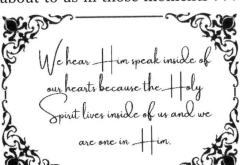

We hear Him speak inside of our hearts because the Holy Spirit lives inside of us and we are one in Him.

just thinking and wanted to say it. It is like we think the same thing at the same time as the other person is thinking. I am so thankful that we hear each other's hearts; how we care about each other, and understand each other's needs.

THE TWO BECAME ONE FLESH

Tanya: Honey, what would you like to say about fulfilling what the Scripture says? Jesus said that the two become one flesh. Also, of course, it was in the beginning in Genesis that the two became one flesh. God Himself says it's a great mystery; so what does that really look like? (Gen 2:24, Mark 10:8).

James: Well, we get the best example when we look in John 17:21 where Jesus is praying. He is talking about how He prays that the church (His disciples) would be one as He and the Father are one. When we think about the relationship which eternally exists within the Triune God—Jesus (the Son), the Holy Spirit, and the Father—three in ONE, it is there that we witness absolute, perfect unity. There's perfect harmony . . . there is no room for darkness; everything is in the light. Within the Godhead a choice is made to stay in their divine character because it is their very identity—distinct but inseparable. Their unified character is peace, kindness, gentleness—the fruit of the Spirit is the central character of God's very nature. Not only is that His expressive fruit He bears; likewise, it is because that is Who He is in every part of His personhood and being (Gal. 5:22-23).

They Shall Become One Flesh by Johann Christoph Arnold (plough.com) states:

"In Hosea 2:19-20 God reveals His love to all people in a special way in the unique bond between husband and wife. In the unique bond of marriage, we discover the deeper meaning of becoming one flesh. Obviously to become one flesh means to become united physically and sexually, but it is far more than that! It is a symbol of a man and a woman bound and melted together, heart, body, and soul, in mutual giving and total oneness."

As von Gagern says, "Often it is only through his wife that the husband becomes truly a man; and through her husband that the wife gains true womanhood." We were created for each other to be one and whole in Christ Jesus.

When I think about the two becoming one in Christ, it is by us choosing to allow God's very nature to be developed in using that oneness like the Father and Son have. If I could say it this way asking God to cement us together in an unbroken relationship, just like the unbroken relationship between the Father and the Son. Yes, I see it also like a triangle of the Father God on the top of the triangle; Jesus on the bottom right of it; and Holy Spirit on the bottom left . . . with my wife and I in the center. It is a triangle, and it says peace on one of its three sides, love (on the bottom as the foundation) and harmony on the side that surrounds us. That will be the picture showing the two becoming one in Christ because really without the Lord we're nothing.

The husband should always take the lead in role modeling to his wife what Christ looks like if Jesus were here in the flesh today. I am convinced as I read the Bible that one of my responsibilities is to become a mirror image of Jesus for my own sake, but also for the sake of my wife; even for my family and everyone around me. Sometimes a wife has an interpretation of the character and nature of God the Father that does not properly resemble Who God is. This will greatly affect the wife's self-image and her interpretation of how God the Father sees her.

Tanya: How should our oneness be, my love? Isn't it the union, the unity of the spirit and soul and body as one in Christ Jesus?

James: Yes, it is, and this certainly indeed is a great mystery. Our oneness should be both practical and spiritual. I am thinking how we raise our kids. It is always important to maintain a oneness, to be on the same page—and on the same child rearing plan. One of the kid's goals, or it seems like at times, is to divide and conquer (1 Cor. 1:10). Have you ever noticed that if one child doesn't get their way with one parent, they run to the other parent and plead their case, without telling that parent that they already got an answer from the other parent, of course! It is of paramount importance for the parents to communicate with each other prior to rendering a decision to the child; maintaining oneness. If not, then the kingdom cannot stand if it is divided (Mark 3:25).

PRAYER KEEPS US ONE

Tanya: I love it when we pray together and pray for one another. **Prayer keeps us together as one.** I always run to God—I pray in good and bad times. The Holy Spirit always strengthens me and gives me wisdom in what to do in each situation.

James, I remember a moment when we had to go to the main hospital (to locate your cancer). I could not come in and stay by your side because of COVID19; but I prayed and kissed you before I left the room. I was praying and practicing our oneness in the Spirit. I went outside to pray—even though I was not in the same room with you, but I was in the same Spirit with you as I prayed over for you.

I have always loved, prayed, blessed, encouraged, while speaking life over you, dear, before you left for your daily radiation treatments which lasted for seven weeks. We're one in Spirit. It is through prayer that we're connected to one another. As I pray for God to bless you and to heal you—I pray for your full recovery and restoration . . . that you be in good health, in excellent condition for His Name's sake, for His Kingdom and glory—that your voice stays fully functional.

I would pray God's Word over you and declare that throughout the day over you the very stripes of Jesus would heal you and make you whole (Isa. 53:5). I prayed that the Lord would do a great work in your life that needs to be done according to His will and plan. We both surrendered to God's will. I see how God really does work it all out for good. Even now as we are writing this book together, we see His hand and good plan for our lives to live and to serve Him and to help many marriages to be truly one. When we pray God hears us and desires that conversation with Him for our spouse.

James: The enemy is always trying to use whatever means he can to bring division within our household—especially, into the marriage of believers in Jesus. When my wife and I pray together, it is not only for the sake of just praying, but it is done intentionally to stand in unity as one for the sake of preserving our marriage identity in Christ Jesus. This goes back to the fall of mankind. One of the enemy's greatest tactics, which is proven to be his most effective, is to isolate an individual in order to get them to question God. If this "accuser of the brethren" can get you to break away from the oneness of the marriage covenant by choosing him, then he knows that he will win that battle most of the time.

This proves to me how important and certainly one of the most paramount activities that a husband should always engage in is being a watchman over his wife. It is exactly why we are to "Wash our Wife daily in the Word"; good communication keeps the deceiver at bay and produces the energy even gaining ground in the relationship. During this communication time the wife can help her husband make wise choices and stay on track. We must protect the sanctity of our marriage covenant. In Philippians 2:2 it says: *"Complete my joy by being of the same mind, having the same love, being in full accord and of one mind."* Be one in everything.

Our union of body, soul and spirit is a representation of being one as the Father, Son and Holy Spirit are one. It was the design of God since the beginning of time before the creation. A few things come to mind. I am a bit of a Nascar fan—there is a lesson to notice from the sport. Most of those cars have about 900 horsepower, a highly tuned suspension, high tech brakes, high performance transmission, a rear axle that is geared just for that track and so on. The driver is a highly skilled person.

Their ability to respond to just about any track condition is profound. Much happens when you are going 200 miles per hour; you travel across a lot of track in about 2 seconds. Like about 600 feet! Yet, if the car and driver do not partner together as one, they are both useless, nor will they ever get to perform the way they were originally designed. All that horsepower and driving skill must become one and work in tandem as one to accomplish great things. Neither can proclaim greatness without the other. **They are humbly dependent on each other as one to become a useful vessel—man and machine!**

Most of us will greatly appreciate what oneness looks like in that Nascar race when the driver faces his fears, becomes one with his Nascar, overcomes all obstacles and challenges, then he crosses the finish line as the winner!

We all celebrate together as we witness what oneness looks like when you have the right partners teaming up together, working as one to become the greatest on the track. We need to live this out in our marriages, as one, so that the Lord is glorified with the win because of His skillful hands on the wheel of our lives.

LEAVE AND CLEAVE

Tanya: Honey, what does leave and cleave mean? I know that many marriages struggle because some husbands call their mom first because of being connected with their mother or the wife has a connection with her mom and dad. They keep trying to be one with someone other than their spouse. The closeness is now misplaced since those affections should now be placed with your spouse as you honor your parents but leave and cleave to your spouse. It affects the relationship of the marriage between the two of them because when they initially got married, they were supposed to be separated physically and emotionally from their parents. It is important that we obey the Word of God which says that you are to leave the parents and cleave to your husband and wife as one flesh (Genesis 2:24).

Dr. Miles Munroe explains that when the wife marries a husband, she leaves her father and transfers to another father which is now her husband as a provider. The husband now provides what her father used to provide financially, emotionally—she is no longer under her father's spiritual covering.

James: It is the physical and emotional act of transferring your love and affection from your parents to your spouse. Dr. Munroe is correct on the above statement. To me, to have the most effective marriage relationship, you cannot have a divided heart. If you are giving the emotions to your parents that you should be giving to your spouse, then it is difficult to cultivate intimacy when your heart is divided. This is a tough issue as some spouses portray their spouse as a controlling person, when in fact we both should equally be committed to protecting our oneness in our marriage, as our first priority.

GREAT MYSTERY

Tanya: I love the words *great mystery* Paul used in Ephesians 5:31. Honey, how do you see that in a marriage covenant?

James: I have a theory—I don't mean it to sound irreverent—that might help with understanding that "Great Mystery." I grew up watching the "Three Stooges." Each one of them have a defined, unique personality. Each one of them have a name: Larry, Curly, and Moe. They will respond to their own names when you call each one out. However, when you shout out *Three Stooges* all three of them can look back and acknowledge you equally because that is who they are, the three are one. It is so similar to that great mystery of the oneness of Father, Son, and Holy Spirit; Three unique personhoods, yet oneness in nature and unity. I know, quit laughing, this illustration you'll never forget!

I know that is one of the things we both appreciate and support in our marriage is protecting our own unique identity.

So, it is in our marriage. When you call out Tanya or James we will respond with the uniqueness of our names. However, should you shout out "Hey Wheelers" both of us can equally respond as Wheelers, as one, because that is who we are. I know that one of the things we both appreciate and support in our marriage is protecting our own unique identity. I want my wife to remain herself, only to become the best version of herself through the sanctification process of the Lord. This should be a representative relationship of what the church looks like. In 1 Corinthians 12:12 onward Paul speaks about how we are members of one body, and yet we are many members, all of us having our own unique identity. In our marriage we are to role model as an example to the church—His living Ekklesia—what that should look like, maintaining our individual character in Christ, yet oneness in the Lord.

In *The Mystery of Marriage* by John Piper—you can listen to his audio too (desiringgod.org)—he says:

"What this implies is that when God engaged to create man and woman and to ordain the union of marriage, He didn't roll the dice or draw straws or flip a coin as to how they might be related to each other. He patterned marriage very purposefully after the relationship between His Son and the Church, which He had planned from all eternity. Therefore, marriage is a mystery. It contains and conceals a meaning far greater than what we see on the outside. God created man both male and female and ordained marriage so that the eternal covenant relationship between Christ and His church would be imaged forth in the marriage union. The inference Paul draws from this mystery is that the roles of husband and wife in marriage are not arbitrarily assigned but are rooted in the distinctive roles of Christ and His church."

This is the mystery of intimacy and oneness we have in a marriage of how Jesus has designed it to be from the beginning of the creation with the Church and in a marriage.

Tanya: Honey, I wanted to ask you about what the Holy Spirit showed you when we come together?

James: One of the purposes of physical intimacy is for husband and wife to become one. Though they are two separate individual people, yet they are one. That's part of the great mystery that Jesus speaks about being one in the marriage. He wants to us to be as a real example; to help us understand a kingdom relationship example of how Jesus and His Father are one yet two separate personhoods (Eph 5:32).

The marriage is to give us an insight of how it is possible that you have the Father and the Son, two different persons, two distinct personalities, two unique expressions of our One God. Yes, they are one—even so the Triune God, with the Holy Spirit. Just as a husband and wife are two different people, two different personalities, two different personhoods; yet they are one. This is the very relationship that Jesus was describing in His prayer, that we would be brought into the oneness of the Father and the Son—we being the Church, we become one with the Father and the Son in their eternal "fellowship" or koinonia as it says in 2 Peter 1:3-4:

> *"His divine power has granted to us all things that pertain to life and godliness, through the knowledge of him who called us to his own glory and excellence, by which he has granted to us his precious and very great promises, so that through them you may become partakers* (lit. "koinonia" or "in fellowship") *with the divine nature; having escaped from the corruption that is in the world because of sinful desire."* (ESV)

31

One of my greatest prayers is that we continue to grow in oneness in marriage, giving no place to the enemy. As a benefit in our marriage, it is an example to the world of the oneness of the Father, the Son, and the Holy Spirit. It is the role model of the oneness that Christ intends between Himself and His Church. It is a oneness of pristine fellowship—we do not become each other—we remain distinct persons, but utterly inseparable.

Tanya: This is the true love about being one as we show godly love to each other. This is a deep and intimate love. This is how God wants to reveal His love to us: God the Father, Jesus the Son, and the Holy Spirit—distinct but inseparable. This represents to me how my husband has such closeness of deep love with me that we have, when we lay on each other's chest and experience deep love; even cry because of the deep love connection. That is really the deep relationship that we, as the Church, should have with the **Father, Jesus, and Holy Spirit as the Trinity, in oneness and fellowship with Him . . . even so, as we are one in our marriage.**

In their *Love and War* book, by John and Stasi Eldredge, they write:

"In some sense marriage is the Kingdom of God, the purpose for which God has been fighting lo these many ages—the marriage of Christ and His Church, that is. All other marriages end here, for God will be united with his people. And so, we see from start to finish, the part of this great story we have been given to play begins and ends with a marriage. Christianity is the greatest love story the world has ever known. Now consider this: Marriage is the sanctuary of the heart." (Ref. p. 26 of *Love and War*)

This portrays unity.

The two are better than one . . . and a *"threefold cord is not quickly broken"* (Ecclesiastes 4:9-12). I love this verse in that it explains how we need each other to be one in marriage, in Christ Jesus. We cannot have a marriage that will last without this reality of the "threefold cord." It is only through God that we have that godly love to give to each other. Otherwise, without that love we cannot experience true unity, union as we are sharing here. It is so powerful. This is our true focus, our identity that we have "in Christ."

SECTION TWO: IDENTITY

I am crucified with Christ, nevertheless I live,

yet not I, but Christ lives in me "

(Gal. 2:20)

OUTSIDE OF CHRIST, I AM WEAK; INSIDE OF CHRIST I AM STRONG.

Chapter 3:
Our Identity & Roles in Christ Jesus

I dentity is the very foundation where everything must start. It is also our greatest weapon against the enemy, but it is also the foundation that will support everything else within the marriage. The truth is when we know who we are in Christ Jesus then we have the clearest understanding of how we should function as a person.

Tanya: Honey, what would you like to say about our identity of who we are?

James: **Our identity is in Christ Jesus.** When we go deeper to understand it we will have the mind of Christ, so we will have that same understanding, the same ability to view things from His perspective and to interpret situations through the lens of His eyes. When we live an intentional life where we are always reflecting Jesus, it is during those moments that we walk with the Father doing what the Father says. Remember Jesus never acted outside of His own authority but always within the authority of His Father—that is the truest identity in Christ.

It is a relationship of submission to the Lordship of Jesus you take on. You put on the very character, that very nature, the very essence of God that flows out of us and inflows to your spouse. *You cannot give your spouse what you do not have yourself.*

It is about walking in your new identity in Christ Jesus as it says in Galatians 2:20: *"I have been crucified with Christ, it is no longer I who live but Christ lives in me . . .."* In 1 Corinthians 6:19-20 it says that we are no longer our own, for we are bought with a price. Who bought us? It was Jesus who bought us, so we ought to live a life of appreciation, glorifying God in all that we do.

Tanya: My example of my personal identity in Christ is this: Because I have experienced and know Jesus' love, it brings me into an understanding of how much I mean and who I am to Him when I spend my time alone with the Lord. God would tell me: "You please Me My daughter, you bring Me pleasure, you are My daughter." My Heavenly Father calls me by my name, Tanya. The Father again says to me: "I love you and I see you complete and whole." This is how He sees me and you too—pure, holy, and so beautiful in His sight, because He sees Jesus inside of us.

I am His bride and His child. I saw myself sitting with my Heavenly Father and Jesus Christ and the Holy Spirit all around us as one. It is so beautiful to see that identity, that oneness with Him and how Father God sees me perfect and complete in Jesus Christ. I have been created in His image and likeness (Genesis 1:27).

The more healing I receive in my heart, and the more revelation of God's Word I see—while listening to good teachings concerning my identity in Christ and the renewing of the mind—have given me the confidence to know who I am in the Lord. I wrote down on my Facebook wall that I am Tanya Wheeler daughter of the Most High God. That is what I say to a lot of people, even to my own children by helping them to know who they are in Christ Jesus—they are the children of God and so are you if you believe Jesus as your Savior.

I remember in college my professor asked me: "Who are you?" I just said it out loud: "I am a child of God." That moment was so powerful, because it helped me understand that the Holy Spirit does live inside of me . . . I am sealed with the Holy Spirit of Promise and I belong to God (2 Corinthians 1:21-22; Ephesians 1:13-14).

In *The Truth of Your Identity* by Kristine Dohner we read:

"You were created in the image of God . . . and He said it was very good. God loves you. And He likes you. Of all the over seven-and-a-half billion people on the Earth, your DNA, fingerprints, and eye prints are different from everyone else. God created you uniquely, with strengths and weaknesses, and He LOVES what He created. *He never makes a mistake.* You are no mishap or fluke of nature. God intended you. He planned for you, and He prescribed every single detail of your body, your race, color of your skin, hair and eye color, and every other feature. In fact, you are His best idea ever!"

Now that is who you are.

Tanya: Honey, I really appreciate that you have a strong identity in Christ. I am so thankful that you have helped me with my identity of who I am in the Lord. What has helped you personally to know and understand your identity? What kind of examples can you share, my love?

James: I think that one of the greatest problems is that men want their identity to be of this world. **It is a choice, and clearly you must choose with whom you want to identify.** We can't just make excuses like: "It's just who I am; it's my culture, and so on." You see, the issue is men have attachments to the things of the world. I am not suggesting that women don't have such attachments to the world, but rather men tend to have a larger issue with pride. From their pride they want to compete against other men and live by the world's standards. They want to be seen as successful, to be ahead of others, to have more than others, to have the bigger truck, the larger house, the Harley-Davidson, the nicest bikes, all the toys, absolutely the largest TV to watch football and other sporting events, and the fastest wave runner, etc.

The confidence that I have in who I am in Christ Jesus—as in "from where does my identity come"—it comes from me spending time with the Lord. I have to be intentional in making plans to get alone and search out the Lord. This would not only include my quiet time with the Lord, but for me it was and is getting away into nature. It was in those quiet moments that I could, and still do, cry out to the Lord and hear Him.

The Holy Spirit is the one Who was calling me and giving me the desire to search for the Lord; but I continually have to make a choice, a conscience effort to meet the Lord in those moments. I've learned how important it is to just open my heart with the Lord and be vulnerable with Him. During those moments I've learned that I can trust Him because He's always proven to me that He has a great plan for my life.

> ➤ *Through many tears of repentance and regret, I found that the Lord always responded in love, never with condemnation.*

Rather, He lovingly wrapped His arms around me and just held me. His loving encouragement gave me the strength and ability to trust Him—to move forward with life. Some of the other practices that I do daily is listening to other mature teachers who speak into my life those messages that are about our identity in Christ. These activities have been such a huge part in laying the foundation of my identity in knowing who I am in Christ Jesus.

OUR ROLES

Tanya: Honey, talking about our roles, how are we supposed to be serving each other? You came to me like Jesus; you came to serve and not to be served. Please expand on what does that look like? *I have learned that the secret to a happy marriage is to be a servant, to please one another.* It is my belief that we need to put aside all selfishness. What are your thoughts?

James: Well, *I wanted a wife, not a servant.* That is the way Jesus sees the Church because we are going to love our wives, as Christ loves the Church (lit. His "Ekklesia") and "gave up Himself for her." Jesus never views the Church as his servant, because remember He says, "I do not call you servants, but I call you My friends." That is the heart attitude

40

of Jesus towards His Church. The heart attitude of a husband towards his wife, his friend, which is someone that you just love to hang out with; not someone with whom you're having a power struggle.

If Jesus really wanted to be competitive with us, obviously, He could—He would always win! You know He spoke, and the entire universe came into existence ("by Him were all things created"—Col. 1:16—ESV), so, He clearly has more power and the upper hand. Too many husbands live a life trying to have the upper hand with their wife, trying to prove to her, out of pride and arrogance, that the male dominates. That fleshly world wants him to prove his masculinity by how much he is in control. This attitude is nothing that Jesus ever called a husband to be. He never acted like that. Jesus never spoke rudely to His Bride. He never cheated. Jesus never treated the Church that way. Rather, He said we are to love one another, to serve one another, and to lift each other up.

Tanya: Why do so many men try to dominate their wives? What should be the primary role of men in their marriages?

James: Well, but to go back to what you are asking, it is this question: Why do men sometimes try to act so tough and in charge? It is the cultural environment. It seems now it is almost like a man has been stripped of his manhood—so, he's out to prove them wrong!

You see, the point is this: A man who has lost his true identity of being confident, and in how to dress well, in the sense that, not just on the outside but on the inside, is trying to be a confident man. He wants to be proud to be a man who walks around with confidence, dressing well, and living a life of servanthood, being a servant by lifting others up. Confusing? Yes, that is what happens when identities get all mixed up.

But to your point, you know, too many men were raised to be tough, not cry any tears. Suck it up. You know, do whatever it takes to get it done. There's a lot of truth to it, but it should never be at the expense of stepping on your wife, and making her feel less because sometimes men forget when they step on their wife they're really stepping on Jesus; because if you have a Christian wife you are stepping on Jesus too.

Remember, God Himself lives in your wife; so when you put down your wife you're putting down the Lord, and when you step on your wife, emotionally, you're stepping on the Lord. Eventually the Lord's going to make the man pay the price. On the one hand, the Lord is exceedingly kind. He is very patient. On the other hand, if you keep stepping on his daughter, He's going let you know He does not appreciate that. Then it becomes, how does the man respond to this?

Tanya: How should man's role be? Do you think a man to be only a provider and not help around the house? Usually a woman cooks and cleans, and the men just provide and, well, that's how people think they are wired.

James: I think, a man, traditionally—the way he is created—feels more like a whole person when he is out working and providing.

But let's look at another scenario. I see a physician's assistant who obviously makes good money while her husband works part time. She was telling me about her pregnancy. They are going to have their first baby and her husband works part time at home; he does not make a lot of money. He's already the guy who takes care of the home front. He takes care of all the chores; does the cooking and cleaning. He's the one who will do the lion's share of raising the baby during the day while she works and brings home the bacon.

It is not right for a man to be so prideful and arrogant. I will go out and work and take care of the family. Oh really, you are a part time guy that you know does not make a lot of money. Your wife is a highly skilled woman that is making more money. So put your gifting to work in the best place where it works.

I think about our situation. I am recovering from a work injury. I make some money, but you make a little more than I do. Yet, we are working to our strengths, as a team, even though I don't really like you working. I know that you're not a big fan of working, but I can't go out and work at full capacity at this moment. So, what can I do? Well, I can keep the house clean, I can do the cooking. I can be at home with the girls. I can pour out a living example of excellence into their lives and into their hearts, into their minds, and just be here for them. We must get rid of that arrogant pride which says: A man's role is only provider. Well, if that is what truly works and is possible and achievable—so be it. If not, then you know you must set your pride aside and look at the practicality of life. What is the best thing that works for our family?

BEING ONE IS TEAMWORK

Tanya: Honey, I really like how we were talking about being one team. I like how you explained to me about football, and how each player shares their roles. Tell me more about it, my love?

James: Right now, it is football season, and I think about the players and their roles. They have a position, however at times they take on a different role so the team can have a successful play. I recently watched a game when the tight end caught some footballs, and even made a touchdown! However, on many plays, he simply blocked for the runner. There were other plays where he carried the ball. He intercepted the ball. He was a team player for the sake of everyone getting to the playoffs successfully for the teams' best interest.

We need to adapt more and more to *a flexible lifestyle* that says, "I'll do whatever I need to do so that all things that need to be done get done." It is what Jesus practiced daily. There were days that He healed the sick and on other days He cast out demons. Then on some days He dealt with the Pharisees and times where He fed thousands of people. Are we doing this in our daily life like Jesus?

Certainly in our own marriage our roles have changed at times. Prior to Covid-19 coming, I typically would work out of our financial office, make appointments, and help people learn to save for a tax-free retirement strategy. My wife assisted me within our business in many ways. We had roles. When Tanya was not helping me, she'd be running our girls around and then taking care of our household chores. When I got home I almost always cooked dinner; and I made breakfast too, because I enjoy cooking as much as I can. Doing laundry, the dishes and cleaning the kitchen, grocery shopping was all part of what I did to help make sure everything got done, and I enjoy doing that. Tanya took care of everything else. Then all of that changed.

In July of 2019 I ripped my right rotator cuff completely apart. That changed everything. My wife now was doing almost everything. Ah, many blessing to my sweet wife. My part? Driving the girls around to where they needed to go—to school, work, and their activities. Both Tanya and I had to adapt to new roles to make sure that things just got done. Thankfully, I have recovered from that injury and we are back to our usual way in taking care of our household, Hallelujah!

Tanya: Honey, I am so thankful for all your hard work that you do in business and in ministry with me. I enjoy how you like cooking and cleaning and doing many chores around the house, and, of course, driving the kids to work. I enjoy encouraging you—I want to be your best cheerleader while ***believing for a better you*** that all your dreams and aspirations come true. I want to love you by helping us to be on the same page.

I see the importance of us working together as one team that helps each other to make things better and to adapt to all the of the rapidly changing plans which seem to happen daily . . . even as we are writing this actual sentence. We work with

44

each other to help each other. We talk about who does what—but we are flexible in making changes as necessary depending on the needs in our changing environment. *Let us choose to live in harmony, peace, and humility instead of competing against each other regarding who does what role* (Luke 9:46-48). Let us teamwork it!

Tanya: Honey, we all have different gifts, talents, and our strengths and weaknesses that we bring to the table, like I am more of a prayer warrior person, and you are a strategic planner. How can we complement and help each other to become a better you?

James: *A man and a woman, a male and a female, this is our truest identity how we were created from the beginning.* We are all free—"*no male nor female*"–we are one in Christ Jesus (Genesis 1:27, Galatians 3:28).

Tanya: Yes, Oh, thank you Jesus. I receive that in Jesus' Name. That is why we are equal in Christ. Amen. Hallelujah. Thank you.

This is a deep topic for husbands who think they are above their wives.

James: The truth is God sees them as equals in Him. Honestly, they are going to be accountable to God. Because like Father God came to Adam, not asking Eve, where are you? He did not come to the wife, Eve. Men sometimes think that they are to rule over their wives. But that is not how it really is. You know when Eve took the forbidden fruit, God did not come looking for Eve—He came looking for Adam. One of the things that has always amazed me is how many men think so arrogantly that they are to rule over their wives.

It is a very humbling position. We as men, are to point our wives and family to the cross. This is out of a place of humility; out of great responsibility that we lead our family to the Lord. It is out of example, because we're called to live it first. Our own testimony, our own lifestyle should point our wife, our family and marriage to the cross. So, it's actually with great humility we stand before the Lord saying: "Give me the grace, the strength, and all that I need to properly lead my wife." Ultimately, the husband must give an account for the results. Remember, Adam was standing next to his wife Eve. Adam failed to protect his wife from the enemy. Eve was deceived—Adam was disobedient . . . there's a big difference. Adam was told upon creation to take authority and subdue. Adam should have taken authority over Satan and protected his wife from the Serpent's deception. In that he miserably failed—Adam was disobedient.

Now, sadly and immediately, Adam tried to blame his wife, instead of taking responsibility—*"the woman you gave me."* That just *proves to me that when we try to blame others, that is the first indication that sin is within us.*

➢ **Because when we blame others, that is a result of sin.**

So, if I am blaming my wife for something, then the issue isn't my wife—the issue is within myself for not taking responsibility for my own actions . . . not being the "covering" which she needs.

PRACTICING MUTUAL SUBMISSION

Tanya: Honey, I see the importance of practicing mutual submission. This is such an important topic for us to talk about in a marriage. Jesus showed us His first love by dying for us because we are His Bride, the Church; therefore, it is easier for the Bride to return respect to Him and to submit to Him. The submission issue is a hard topic. I see in our society women are the ones who have to submit all the time to men.

Men do not love their wives as Christ loves the Church, His Bride. Or, the opposite, where the wife controls the man.

Wives pray and fast and do good things to win their husbands over for Jesus to change them; some do and some change later, which makes the marriage journey tough. From the beginning it was totally different how it was supposed to be from creation with Adam and Eve. They both were supposed to take dominion and oversee the garden. (Genesis 1: 26). At the beginning, it was all correct. Now it is just sad to see it so distorted. Honey, what do you see in this area of submission or mutual submission?

James: Well, I see, the husband is always responsible. He must take the responsibility to set the pace. Here is what I mean. A husband should first be a role model to his wife. He is to manifest the character of God. This means as a husband, he is to love his wife, as Christ loves the Church. I need to be an example of that. What does that look like? What does godly love look like? What must be created is an environment where *my* wife's submitting to her *own* husband. She has no struggles of submitting to her own husband, because they know that all his motives and his intentions are pure, and good. Why? Because he is for her best interest—for the best interest of the marriage.

The issue which I have is when men don't set the example; then women feel like they have to follow *that Bible verse*, which is so inaccurately interpreted that wives submit to their husbands as unto the Lord (Ephesians 5:22). That does not include when he is a jerk, because I am not into enabling jerks. If a wife submits to her husband who's a jerk and allows the abuse, then they do not give the husband any reason to change. The man thinks: "She submits to me, while I'm being a dysfunctional jerk. Why should I change?" I don't think so.

No. We should not enable bad behavior either. No matter what, a husband has no excuse for refusing to take responsibility to do what he knows he should do before the

Lord, and in his own personal walk with the Lord. His first responsibility is to love the Lord his God with all his heart, soul, mind, and strength. The second is to love his wife, as Christ loves the church. That is the first responsibility of a husband in the natural. There is just no way to excuse a husband's dysfunctional behavior. Why? If a husband is truly a follower of Christ, then he cannot say I am a Christian, and yet dishonor his wife. It just does not work that way. I will challenge any husband in half a heartbeat: How can you call yourself a Christian, if in fact you are not loving your wife as Christ loves the Church?

Tanya: Yes. This is true. This is why it's so important in getting this right from the get-go if a couple wants to have a healthy relationship, a healthy marriage. It is important that there is genuine love and respect in a godly way in the marriage affecting every area of married life. I know that there are marriages where God may be using a woman to save the man, but it is ultimately Christ Who does the saving.

That is why it is easier to be equally yoked right away. Healing and restoration should be a couple's reality before they get married. I know such a "reality" can be workable in the marriage when it is kind of dysfunctional. Anything is possible with the Lord, but it is better to start out correctly, when both parties are healed and made whole prior to tying the knot.

James: Yes sweetie, anything is possible! *Part of the solution to this issue comes down to this: Will a man be willing to bend his knees, his will, to the Lordship of Jesus Christ?* This is and must be the starting place: the cross!

> ➤ **It's only upon complete surrender that the Holy Spirit is now free to coach you, to teach and transform you.**

Mostly for me, it was also when I spent time reading the Word of God on a very regular basis. I had to get to know God. To allow His word to begin transforming the way that I think.

48

As it says in Romans 12:2, we must start with our mind. How we think and perceive things upon the first inception of any thought. It is how we process that thought from that point that determines the outcome. With a mind that is ruled by Christ, the thought becomes a godly thought which produces a godly response and action.

Tanya: What is the right order and who is supposed to be the leader?

James: My interpretation of the head of the house is perhaps a little different than others; what I mean by that is *I am not to rule over my wife and command her to submit to me.* What it really means to me is that it is my responsibility as a husband to set the pace and the spiritual temperature in the home to be the head defined as giving direction under the anointing and leading of the Holy Spirit. I am to be the spiritual eyes—to be a watchman over my family. I'm to have the spiritual eyes to see what Father God is doing, just as Jesus said I only do what I see the Father doing (John 5:19).

I pray and ask the Father what do You want me to do in my marriage? As the head I need to think like Jesus thinks; I need to hear the voice of the Holy Spirit so I can receive instruction and direction for my family.

Tanya: Honey, do you have the last word to say? Because you are the responsible one for me as your wife and for our children, right? So then you're the one that's kind of really in charge, I mean the Lord is in charge and the head of you, then you're supposed to be over me and together we are over our kids, right? Isn't that kind of like the order in God's Kingdom?

James: There's always an order. So, to answer your question: Ultimately, the Lord will always come to the husband and encourage the husband to give an account for what takes place in the family. The greatest example for this of course is in the Garden of Eden. I also think about King David. When David sinned, the Lord did not go to the woman with whom David slept, He went to David and made David give an accounting of his actions. Yes, that's a little different situation but there's multiple examples in the Bible where the Lord goes to the man of the house, not to the woman of the house, to confront the man only for the sake of bringing necessary repentance and instruction.

Tanya: Right, because you are my husband, you are my covering and you are the protection of the home so you're basically the leader of the house, the head of the house but not in a bossy way. You know, you're not to control by asserting dominion over me because we are equal in Christ, right?

James: Correct—we are equally yoked or equal and yet I do have a role that says I'm ultimately responsible as the head and as the leader to be in authority under the direction of the Holy Spirit in leading my family in the direction that I believe God wants us to lead. God is the source Who gives me the direction to be the head of my family.

The crucial part here is what happens when the husband gets it wrong? In my experience, too many wives will beat their husbands up emotionally about their shortcomings. See, during the time when a husband makes a final decision because he believes this is what the Lord wants him to do for his family, his wife—yet, he gets it wrong—then her response should be: "It's OK; God's hand is upon my husband and if my husband doesn't get it right, I'm going to choose to love him and pray for him. In fact, I will continue to pray for him during this season. *I am submitting to his leadership in the head position that my husband scripturally has.*"

How important it is that a wife prays for her husband. If he's right, there is unity because as an act of love she's praying for her husband not to wake him up because she has a point to prove, but to pray that the Holy Spirit continues to communicate to the husband so if there needs to be adjustments and changes the Holy Spirit Himself will get the husband's attention and bring those corrections and conviction.

Then the wife can rejoice knowing that God fought my battles. It doesn't bring disruption to the marriage because that's what Satan would want to do is to bring division with pride: "See, I told you I was right!" That's the kind of attitude that is totally opposite the Lord's disposition.

This is why God wants us to have the right attitude and character and heart. In my cultural background we were taught to have the man be in control and to dominate. The wife was to submit without questioning him no matter what, which is not Christ-like or scriptural. Now, if we mess up, we apologize and give each other grace to understand. We come into unity and love by both of us submitting to the Lord.

Tanya: Honey, what are your final thoughts and steps which couples can take in knowing their truest identity?

James: We are created in the image of God. He placed within us His very nature, His presence through Holy Spirit is within us. Just that alone has a huge impact on our identity. That makes life not only exciting, but all things truly become possible.

If you are struggling with your identity or how to change, then let us look at some possible action steps to take.

1. Pray (e.g. *"I pray for a spirit of conviction, spirit of repentance, spirit of salvation – to help them come to the truth, the light, and their senses . . .."* – Ref. 2 Tim. 2:25-26)

2. Pray-Read the Bible (2 Tim. 2:15) – *"Holy Spirit illuminate Your Word to me from the pages of this Book . . . I come to You, Lord Jesus, and pray I see You and rightly divide Your Word in me!"*

3. Get to church and around mature healthy couples

4. Counseling and inner healing

5. "Me time"—we will explain more in the workbook

Ultimately, Jesus is the perfect role model of how we should view ourselves. We should daily look into the mirror and ask, just like David did: *"Search me, O Lord, and know my heart and see if there is anything in my life and heart that isn't pleasing to you"* (Psalm 139:23-24). Jesus said *"For where your treasure is, there your heart will be also"* (Matthew 6:21). So, it begs the question of where is your treasure? If you treasure who you are as a follower of Jesus, then you will find contentment in this life no matter what you have or don't have. If your treasure is your stuff, then you might want to rethink who is really the Lord of your life. If you should lose your stuff, will you lose yourself because the stuff was your identity? If your identity is in Christ and your treasure is in heaven, then your ability to walk in peace is possible because you understand stewardship—where your identity truly is and who you are in Christ Jesus.

One of the greatest moments for me is when I lost everything, and I realized that I have everything that I will ever need. I have the Lord. I have an amazing wife. I have awesome kids and grandkids. I have life in my body. I can serve in our ministry. I am truly blessed.

Gratitude for what we do have is the best platform for understanding who you are in Christ and keeping our priorities in check with kingdom values.

Chapter 4
Woman, Wife, Mom, Friend, Daughter

Knowing your identity as a woman, a wife, a mom, a friend, and daughter is powerful. These are the steps of development of first knowing and loving who you are as a woman, then you become a wife if God has called you to be married; then you may find yourself in a loving mother's role. You'll find yourself gathered with true friendship—first, you will become a daughter to God and a daughter to your parents. You will become this amazing combination of identities wrapped in one . . . this is who you were created to be. Not everyone can be a wife or mother, but know this: You will always be a woman, a friend, and a daughter.

A WOMAN

Tanya: Honey, what's your view on how a real, true, confident woman should act?

James: A confident woman is a woman who is absolutely a secure woman who is not afraid to speak her heart and her mind. All our behaviors and actions should be from a platform of godly character, based upon a foundation of godly love. That confidence gives her the boldness to be 100% herself; how Christ created her to be. Remember, it is because the kingdom of God lives in us that confidence should reflect the confidence of Jesus, because Jesus was a brilliantly confident man.

All our behaviors and actions should be from a platform of Godly character, based upon a foundation of Godly love.

He was very gentle, but He was bold as He walked into every situation; He knew exactly what to do.

Tanya: Yes, Honey, it is just so important to know how we are created as a woman. One of my favorite books and authors to read is called *Captivating* by John and Stasi Eldredge; they write:

> "So, may we take a moment and remind you who you truly are? You are a woman. An image bearer of God. The Crown of Creation. You were chosen before time and space, and you are wholly and dearly loved. *You are sought after, pursued, romanced, the passionate desire of your Fiancé, Jesus.* You are dangerous in your beauty and your life-giving power. And you are needed." (page 217)

This is who you are. The beauty of a woman is inside of us to shine forth to the world so that people can see that rest and peace in our lives that especially benefits our husbands, our families, and everybody around us.

A WIFE

Tanya: I just got a deep inside revelation. Wow! I am doing, and obeying, and respecting and submitting to my husband, as unto the Lord Jesus Christ Himself. It is so powerful because I struggle with submitting, listening or hearing my husband. It seems to go into one ear and out the other. **Listening by seeking understanding—not just answering back.** I truly just need to really honor him and love him as unto to the Lord. In Ephesians 5:21 it says: "Submit to one another out of reverence for Christ." Therefore, we ought to practice mutual submission because we are submitting to the Lord.

We do it out of love and honor by the Spirit of God, not based on performance or duties. For men, respect and submission makes them feel loved and honored. It is believing and trusting in them and in their dreams and visions. We as wives are to pray, come alongside our husbands by encouraging and obeying them out of love.

Honey, thank you for genuinely loving me as the Lord loves the Church. It is easy for me to want to respect and honor you back. I am doing this as unto Jesus Christ Himself. *It is a joy to give my myself to you, my love.* I am just so thankful that I can enjoy you and be fully with you in my mind, my soul, my emotions, my feelings, my **whole heart**—just everything to fully give you my all. This is an amazingly and beautiful picture of how Jesus' love is shown to and through us.

This is such a deep revelation and insight into the mystery of how a wife is supposed to align herself with her husband and how she is supposed to honor him, love him, and give herself fully to him. Our spiritual mom, Mary, told us before our marriage to honor each other as unto the Lord. I always think about practicing and choosing love as my sole response in respecting and honoring my husband.

Tanya: Honey, in what areas can the wife help her husband?

James: I can only answer from my own perspective and experience, but I think it is probably true for most men. To feel respected, listened to, accepted, desired, and valued by their wife empowers them. When one's wife pours this into their relationship, then the husband feels like they can walk on water and conquer the world around them.

The opposite is also true. When we do not experience those affirmative relationships, we tend to withdraw, close up, and potentially fall into seeking those things outside of the marriage.

If a man always feels put down—not being able to satisfy her—well, most of the time he becomes emotionally vulnerable. This can lead to an opening for the enemy of our souls to send a woman into his life who will gladly make him feel accepted, respected, and even loved—but this is a trap.

I know that when the proverbial bar is always being raised, it causes many men to basically say, "Fine, I am not willing to put any more effort into that anymore because I never get the *appreciated* response." Of course, it's a two-way street.

I believe the husband needs to be the leader in the marriage and the affirmative role model to his wife. What that looks like has everything to do with himself pouring in those affirmations into the marriage. On the one hand, he should communicate kindly and clearly with his wife before marriage what his needs are; on the other hand, she ought to communicate what her needs are as well. Position yourself for victory, for success in the beginning!

PREPARATION SEASON

Tanya: Because I allow the Lord to heal me, to recover me, to restore me, I find my love in Jesus first. First and foremost, He's my husband, my provider, *my everything*. When James came into my life, I so appreciated that aspect reflected in him—just like Jesus as my eternal Husband. Because I saw and continue to see Christ in him it was a wonderful transference of the Lord's life, care, and love for me that I could now see in my husband—even when I was not married, but certainly as I entered into married life.

My destiny is in Revelations 21:9 "Come, I will show you the Woman, the Lamb's wife" (NKJV side margin). I/we am/are Jesus' Bride. I am in the Lamb's Bride first and foremost—then James, in that order, lest he become my idol. The big change that happened for me was when I read in Isaiah 54:5: "For your Maker is your husband . . .." I started looking to Jesus, the "heavenly Man" (1 Cor. 15:48-49) as my husband before I met my earthly husband.

Today as I am writing this chapter I see how the Lord has been preparing me to become the wife that He has called me to be for the right husband to help him with His dreams and aspirations. It has taken me eight years to walk through a long and deep process of healing in my heart from my past, and renewing of my mind to be in a right place to respect, honor, serve and give my love to my husband.

I had to protect myself, my heart, mind and body from the wrong man and be kept like that ring inside the jewelry store shelf for the right soul mate husband—the man of God who would be perfect for me and I for him. After being faithful to the Lord, while trusting and waiting for God's plan to unfold, then all the pieces came together to bring me the right husband at the right time. God brought him to me. We are a healing balm to each other; now, by God's grace, to many marriages. God can do this for you too and even more.

Tanya: My love, this morning as we were together in bed you told me your deepest heart as you laid on my chest, what was that?

James: So many women are strong willed. I needed a wife who is soft and gentle with me to feel safe, at rest. One who would love and accept me by helping me to become all that I need as a man. Typically, a man has his battles during the day. The last thing he wants is to come home and have the battle continue. This causes a man to delay or avoid coming home. But when I've been fair to you and our marriage by opening up how I feel and by telling you what I need, then I give you the opportunity to respond in love to help me in those moments of need. It is not fair for a man to expect his wife to meet his needs or a wife to expect the same from her husband, if he is not telling his wife what are his immediate needs. You have positioned the marriage for division and have made room for the enemy to creep in if you hold back your true feelings.

Tanya: Yes, my love. I love how we always say, "I love to love you and I love being loved by you." I love your text that you sent me this morning:

James: Good morning my love ♥ 😊 I am so thankful to the Lord that you are so patient with me as I develop as a husband. You encourage me so much when you pray for me, love and accept me, and allow me the freedom of practicing being a good husband. I pray that I continue to grow in the Lord for my sake, for our marriage, for our family and for others. Thank you for your warm and loving embrace 😊 love you sweetie 😳 ♥ 🍃 😿 ♥ 🍃.

Tanya: Good morning, my love ♥, oh it is so sweet to get texts from you especially at 8:31 pm when you are alive and doing well. Thank You Jesus! I'm just so happy, Honey, that God is teaching me to be humble and to love truly love you with sincerity and not out of selfish desires like always wanting my way and having everything on my clock. I thank God even for this cancer situation. It brought me so much closer in understanding you. By helping you and taking care of you I have learned not to satisfy myself but to serve and honor you in your hour of crisis. It means so much to me to be willing and able to love and serve you at this time. Honey, just to love on you and you in return wanting to be with me with the touch of your big hands over my countenance. I love embracing you every time. I love our morning intimacy together. It's so deep . . . it's what the Lord wants us to have with Him as well. This is the expression of His deep love, so beautiful, an image of real love we have in our marriage. It reflects upon our children and upon the world around us. They can see and anticipate that same love surrounding them! It is wonderful to share with others what we have gone through. I love you so much and thank you for loving me so much by being so selfless.

The needs of a woman are to be assured and confident in knowing she is loved by God and her husband. *Marital Intelligence,* by Gil Stieglitz, explains:

> ". . . that wife's needs are honor, understanding, security, building unity, agreement, nurture, and defender. Husband's needs are respect, adaptation, domestic leadership, intimacy, companionship, attractive soul and body, and listener (page 170)."

A woman wants a man with a good heart and good moral character while being a spiritual leader. A man wants a woman who affirms, appreciates, and believes in him and his vision. We pray for others in their marriage relationships that both husband and wife will be able to meet the needs of each other through the help of the Holy Spirit.

A MOTHER'S ROLE

A mother's heart is nourishing, loving, gentle, tender, soft, patient, understanding, teaching, and protective of her children. *Like nature how the mamma bear protects her baby bear cubs.* I remember as a single mom being like a momma bear so protective over them. I have learned to give them into God's hands to cover and protect them. For God loves our children more than we do. We must let them go so God can work with and inside of their hearts.

> ➢ **Prayer is the most powerful thing we can do.**

I remember with my oldest daughter going through a most difficult time. The Holy Spirit continues to teach me to fully depend on Him for everything--only He can change my daughter's heart. I've told this to so many of my close friends and associates. First, I had to change the inside of my heart and mind, by forgiving and letting things go, while choosing to unconditionally love her with my husband at my side while truly trusting in God for her. When I gave up all my efforts— that is when the Lord brought her safely home. The Holy Spirit did the work deep inside her heart. Let us depend on Holy Spirit for everything to change, heal, fix, restore, bring about, and make it all new. I pray that for everyone reading this book.

I love how the Lord continues to show and teach me His love as a Father cares for His children through our own children. I appreciate that the most. I have struggled in this area, but by the grace of the Lord I have fully accepted my children as God's plan, blessing and gifts from Him. Thank You, Jesus! I know the many struggles that a mother has in raising her children in this society, but I have learned that the more we allow God to change and heal us He will do amazing work in our children too. "Just trust Him!" I say this first to myself.

A FRIEND

I want to thank my Pastor, Sergey Vitukov, who has helped my soul to get well and become strong in the Lord. *When we as men and woman know our identity and our roles—who we really were created to be—it changes everything . . . the whole world.* I am thankful for the many friends God has used in my life. I have learned and prayed for caring friends who would be Spirit-filled and with a heart of love for the Lord. We all need this kind of community surrounding us.

As a woman, wife, mom, friend, and daughter . . . or dad, husband, brother . . . both husband and wife should be simultaneously familiar with all sorts of these roles and behaviors. It's all contingent upon where we are and how we respond in a moment's notice, whatever the occasion. As a sister or brother—on a friendship level—you can go deeper in your familial relationship. Sometimes I as wife want to act as a child. I just want to play, rest, be happy and just have fun with my husband and my children. It is a combination of the harmony in all five areas: woman, wife, mom, friend, and daughter.

All five areas comprise the whole of you. You are living out all these responsibilities. We must develop and mature in order to pass on our experiences how we have been healed and made whole in each of these relational areas.

Some people are able to adapt; to change quickly by God's grace both in heart and behavior, in any given situation . . . willing to allow the Holy Spirit to minister to us by raising us up in those areas to become a reflection of the Lord: more refined, stronger, and more whole.

> ➢ **Spiritual growth does not have time limit**.

Some grow up quicker in their walk of life than others.

A DAUGTHER

First, I know who I am: I am the daughter of the Most High God, my Heavenly Father, Who has created me in His image and has been my everlasting parent. I love my Heavenly Father's embrace; He always welcomes me as I come running to Him and sitting with Him by laying my head upon His chest. I abide in Him; He is that secure and safest place. I am thankful, truly honored, by my mom and dad who have given me life. I pray they live long and healthy lives.

I enjoy declaring and speaking who I am in Christ Jesus. I am healed, restored, and redeemed. I'm in Christ as part of His New Creation. I am that Woman destined to share His love and affection for all eternity as His Beloved Bride and Wife. I am a child of God who has been born again. I am accepted in the beloved and unconditionally loved by Him. I gifted by Him to be creative, a dancer, a prayer warrior, writer, author, mother, mentor, coach, and a wife to my amazing husband, James Wheeler. That's me—that's who I truly am!

I know who I am. I am strong in Him . . . I love who I am and who He has created me to be. I only want to be a better version of myself. Yes, someone who has been individually and uniquely created in Christ Jesus. He has designed me to be perfect, transformed to His Image. I am the Proverb's 31 woman. I am Royalty—a daughter of the King of kings— clothed in His righteousness, made whole, and forever cherished.

JOURNEY OF PROCESS

I have learned to focus on the New Creation aspects in being a woman of God. Yes, I am redeemed and what you see is Tanya made whole, healed by the Lord Jesus. *Instead of focusing on anger, I now focus on how to be gentle, kind, and loving.* As I, you too, can ask the Holy Spirit to help you to change you. It's a process and takes time, but He does hear our prayers. There are many methods or tools which equip us for inner healing and deliverance. Indeed, I have been privileged to attend many workshops on inner healing and deliverance—classes which have been marvelous guideposts along the way where I have learned to mature in my walk with Christ. To all my "sisters" out there . . . Ladies, it is a long process; don't be too hard on yourself. The Holy Spirit is the best Helper. Only He can profoundly change us, our family, and situations for our good, even our best.

Songs: Before writing this chapter, I turned on *Pandora*. This song came up which reminded and touched me so deeply: *How He Loves Us So* by David Crowder and Julie True. It has helped me to sleep and rest in His complete peace.

I asked God for His gift of wisdom, understanding, discernment, interpretation, clarity, and His perfect will and plan. I have learned a hard lesson that it is selfish to want my way, my plan, and my time sequence. I was so resistant with God to force my wants on Him, my expectations, and in my time allotment. Once I did that I lost His peace and joy.

After I repented and surrendered everything to the Lord, I accepted His plan and His way for my life. It was only then that He brought me so much peace and joy—true harmony in my heart. It all began when I was willing for **God to change me—it is about the condition of my heart.** God wants to work on first before He can answer and make the changes surrounding us. I have learned to set healthy boundaries and to be aware of knowing my limits with everyone. That has helped me gain my peace and confidence in virtually all my relationships. Also, it frees me from toxic relationships.

EXAMPLES OF AN OVERCOMER WARRIOR

I would say: "Lord, I choose to let go and trust You and Your plan. I release this pain to You; help me. What am I missing?" He would reply: "Love, peace, etc." Today as I am writing I realize how we need to deal with the lies which originate from the Pit—sent by the enemy of my soul . . . I *renounce* them all and cling to the truth of who I am in Christ. Yes, I renounce any agreement I have had with the lie that I am not good enough . . . instead, dear Lord, I choose to believe Your truth. When I inquire as to the truth about this or that, I am keen to wait, pray and listen to the Holy Spirit's still small voice in my spirit speak to me and say, "You are My daughter and I have chosen you, for you are Mine." Practice this each time you struggle with your thoughts when you sense you are losing His peace—do so by praying over uplifting Scriptures and He will overcome in you!

I have written many journals. I use these abbreviations: God Speak (G/S); Experience (Exp); Learned (Lea); Prayers (P); and Revelation (Rev or I use "*" for important). I started using different colors Red for G/S, etc. Looking back through my journal in the year 2017, I wrote a prayer (P): "Thank you for changing my desire to be more as You are, Lord Jesus; to think and see Your way. God Spoke (G/S): "I hear your prayers . . .then I experienced the presence of God (Exp). That is the most precious manifestation in my life—to be known by God and to know God intimately . . . that's all I'll ever need. (Rev). This the foundation of my life. Yes, and Amen!

I just wrote down all that I processed in that moment. I love, enjoy, and embrace all the *treasures* of learning and maturing to become that woman God has chosen me to be. What a journey this is! "Lord, Your love is enough for me . . . I am secure in Your love."

Dear fellow soul on the journey, I pray your experience is enriched by many encounters with the Lord . . . to get to know him on your road to Emmaus (Luke 24:13-27)—especially, when your hope is lost, your dreams crushed. Let me tell you. He will show up . . . He will open those things concerning Himself in the "Law of Moses and the Prophets and the Psalms concerning Himself." Then your heart will burn within you and you will rush to other disciples . . . you will go to your Jerusalem with great joy . . . praising and blessing God

. . . for you have had your eyes opened to see Who He really is: The God of Resurrection!

Tanya: Honey, yesterday I was struggling inside of my mind and heart and you as my husband acted as a Pastor by declaring something to me . . . what did you say again, my love?

James:

➤ Declare who you are—your identity in Christ

I am the daughter of the Most High God, I am purchased and covered with the blood of Jesus, my body is the temple of the Holy Spirit, my name is written in the Lamb's book of life . . . I belong to God. This speaking will shut the enemy down because you are bringing into the light the darkness. You can pray as it says in Zechariah: "The Lord rebuke you Satan!" (Zech. 3:2) or pray firmly out loud: "I rebuke you, Devil, get behind me . . . I cast you out to the pit!" (Matt. 16:23)

Tanya: Thank you for reminding me to understand deeper of who I am and how to overcome in being "strong in the Lord" . . . to be a confident woman of God. I love declaring who I am out loud or in my mind or read it on my wall: I have been created in the image of God. I am made righteous in Christ and I am made perfect in His righteousness. I can do all things through Christ Who gives me strength (Phil. 4:13).

Many of my struggles—I know many women are comparing themselves with other people . . . but please, cease to worry about what people think. Seizing upon jealousy and envy, desiring to have what others have and you do not, breeds misunderstanding and miscommunication between you and your spouse, between husbands and family.

Our negative self-image is nothing more than the expression of the outward who is decaying day by day—yes, with all the negative thinking, feelings, and hurtful words which destroy (2 Cor. 4:16) but our true "inward man is being renewed day by day!" Fear of intimacy or the unknown future—all are part and parcel of that "old man" that has been crucified with Christ. Complaining and arguing with God and others has been nailed to His Cross! "Lord, I pray, change and help us to see You and ourselves enveloped in Your Love."

It is my own resistance to God when I seek my own way and plan. I had to learn to surrender everything to the Lord to have it be His way as He has planned it all for me in Psalm 139: 16: *"His eyes saw me before I was born."* Every day of my life was recorded. Every moment was laid out before a single day had passed. I had to die first to myself, to my own interests, and fully accept God's plan and ways for me to be the Lord of my life. I am not my own I belong to Him . . . "it is no longer I that live but Christ Who lives in me" (Galatians 2:20). When we/I fully surrendered my whole life to the Lord, then is when His peace and joy came rushing in . . . that's what lasts and bears fruit.

I am first a woman who God has made me to be. Then if I marry, I become a wife, and if I am blessed to have children, I become a mother. I am a friend to many people. I am a daughter to my parents. I am a daughter of the Most High God, my Heavenly Father. We can be loving wives by choosing to respect our husbands because when we respect our husbands by expressing real belief and trust in him, then that is what real love means to them. We will help our husbands to become the leaders God has called them to be. Be Who I am, *Be Me,* Tanya myself, who affirms my husband to be all that he can be in our wonderful Lord and Savior!

The Lord has been preparing me for many years, even decades, to come to this place so that the things that He has taught me, as I look back through my journals, I have heard His voice speaking deeply to me . . . trust me daughter for He will do the same for you . . .

> ➢ **The truest success is the inner peace inside of my heart and mind—not money and other things outside.**

65

God's plans are a lot better for me than anything else. God said I am with you always, I love you. Do not fear or worry about anything This is having a real relationship with God.

The Holy Spirit is the most important one to help us in this world. He lives inside of us. He is the best helper, teacher, comforter, counselor, and strengthener that you'll ever need. When I was a single mom. I could sense His arms around me on several occasions—showing me He was helping me along this journey. He is greater than my husband; greater than anyone here. He is my leader, guide, mentor—all that I need; all that I could ask for . . . I just go to Him; He is my rock, my fortress, my high tower . . . *my Companion and my best Friend—my everything I need!*

Today, how blessed am I to let go. When I was writing down the words in these journals, I now realize how beautiful it is to reflect and see how God had been changing me, growing me by His grace to make me who I am today: an amazing, strong, confident, beautiful woman of God and of faith lead by His Spirit. No, in Him there is no pride here—His care and love are pristine. My boast is in Him! The process of learning and experiencing God's unconditional love has healed and saved me. Praise Him, He has brought me through many storms, crises, pain, disappointment, discouragement, depression, fear, worry, and anxiety. Yes! I now enjoy: "Life and more abundantly!"

Prayer

O how You love me - I have no words my Lord
to say You have won my heart my Lord.
I am so thankful for Your unconditional love that is so
pure, holy, righteous, true, so never ending.
Thank You Lord for bringing me together with my
amazing husband to this place where we can share Your love
with many people who will read this *amazing love story
journey* that You have given us and shown us, to touch many
readers, marriages, singles, divorced, single moms and dads.
Thank You for allowing us to walk through so many
difficult situations in our lives so we can understand having
compassion and loving people where they are.
We love You, precious Jesus, and give You all the glory
honor, and praise forever. Amen.

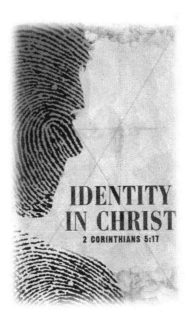

We *love*
because
he first
loved us.

1 John 4:19

Chapter 5
Man, Husband, Dad, Friend, Son

There is hope in becoming the man, husband, dad, friend, and son in His Christ-like Image. If you receive the revelation and experience inside of your heart to become everything that the Lord has called you to be, then you will see a real change inside of you—it will affect every area of your life, especially with your wife.

It is a maturing process where you become who you can be, who you really are . . . it is that *longing to want to change* and be changed into the man that God truly desires you to be. We are called and named His children. We have become His children through the new birth—by believing "into" His Name . . . by "receiving Him" (John 1:12). Our "personhood" has changed—we are now "children of God"— we have been given the "authority" to become the very children of God. Your wife will see that real change from the inside of you—it's "Life-changing." She will honor and respect you and become more of a woman and wife that you have always dreamed she could and would be.

A MAN

Tanya: Honey, I think knowing who you are first as a man is so important. The real issue and question that needs to be answered is why men have not taken up their position, to take their right place as a leader at home and in among God's people. What is the cause, why are men not fully developed as they are called to be?

James: I think those reasons are many; but some of them are as follows:

> ➢ Not dealing with hurts of the past.
> ➢ Not taking your Christian walk seriously.
> ➢ Not willing to set aside your desires for the world.
> ➢ Not dealing with how your dad and/or mom hurt you.
> ➢ Not being healed from being hurt from churches and other Christians.

As you can see, the common theme here is: We need to deal with the hurt in our hearts. The great news is and perhaps the

best news is this: The Holy Spirit is willing and able to completely heal all of us. Jesus paid the price out of love. One of His greatest desires is that we come to personally know how much He wants to heal us. We need to focus on the fact that we have been redeemed and are in the *sanctification process*—that is where we need to be on a regular basis.

One of the things that healed my heart the most was when I saw my dad the way Jesus sees him. Jesus showed me through the lens of how He perceives someone . . . what a man looks like through His lens when that man is submitted to the world and the enemy and not to the Lord Jesus. So, my dad was under the influence of the enemy. My heart was broken for my dad—like this is not his fault. I needed to show my dad the love of Jesus by forgiving him . . . not reacting to my dad's toxic behaviors.

One thing that I have found to be true over my entire life is this: When I say, "Here am I Lord, please help and heal the wounds of my heart and deliver me from those things that torture me." It is here I find Him to lovingly—with full compassion—deliver me from all of those negative things . . . no condemnation, but a loving Savior who saves me.

Once that healing takes place, once we take responsibility to get well, then we are in the proper mindset to take our proper place. This is what happened to me in my own life experience.

Tanya: What is the next step to know? I hear about it from women that their men try to be a leader, but it does not work out. They have little idea why. Maybe it is their story, mindset, or the brokenness that is inside them from past trauma—that pain that needs to be dealt with on a personal level.

James: Men can become leaders of men. I know it is my responsibility to love my wife—to *decide* to make myself do it. Maybe I should reach out and get some "leadership help" outside my own "interior efforts"? We can go to seminars and conferences to gain a greater understanding of these matters regarding leadership or being the leader in your household but then after a few failures you get more discouraged. **You feel empty because you can know what to do and what not to do, but you can get more discouraged and feel empty because you can feel so condemned in that you know that you're reacting out of pain.**

It is good to know who you want to be and force yourself to reach out. Focusing on deeds and works, sure, but if you don't know your full identity of who you are . . . have a vision to possess the character, the essence, and the nature of what a true man of God should be—you'll continue to come up short. If in your *heart* you still do not love your wife, then really nothing matters insofar as what you try to do—you'll just go back to your old ways.

If you are willing to change then the solution will begin with prayer—welcoming and allowing the Holy Spirit to give you a change of heart from the inside out. Then, and then only, will you have that heart of love for your wife. *Only God can do that if you fully are willing to surrender your heart to the Lord to do that deep work inside of you.* You have to go through a process of dying to self by allowing God to break down your fleshly efforts; die to your stubborn will; kill all of the arrogance and pride; your worldly ways; your pornography, anger—it's time to replace your SELF, bring it to His cross and fill it up with God's love to bear all nine fruits of His nature as found in Galatians 5:22-23:

> "... *the fruit of the Spirit is love, joy, peace, longsuffering, kindness, goodness, faithfulness, gentleness, self-control . . . Against such there is no law.*"

> ➤ **There is a difference between knowing and being.**

The example is when my son was born; yes, I *knew* then and there that I became a dad. I had that title, that name, but to *be* a dad is a process of growth and development in which I fully became a father to my son for every son needs a true father.

A HUSBAND

Tanya: Honey, in your Session: Man, Husband, dad, and Friend, is there something you would like to add to that brief title—like how do you really identity as a "man." There's a perception that says to be a real man you have to be some kind of tough, abrasive, even insensitive guy to be a real man. I've often heard: "Real men don't cry . . . they just strap up their boots, get on that horse, ride the herd, etc. . . . really, that's the perception that the world views what constitutes a real man and/or that's the best perception of a "man" out there. Can you clarify what that perception is all about?

James: What clearly defines a real man has everything to do with loving your wife as Christ loves His Church—that alone constitutes a real man, a real husband.

When you understand the role into which a man is called, then you have no alternative—you will be gentle and loving.

Listen up everyone: "Husbands love your wives and do not be harsh with them" (Col. 3:19 – Berean Study Bible). "Cut 'um off and your prayers, to say the least, will be greatly hindered" . . .

*"Likewise, husbands, live with your wives in an understanding way, showing honor to the woman as the weaker vessel, since they are heirs with you of the grace of life, **so that your prayers may not be hindered**"* (1 Pet. 3:7—English Standard Version)

We are called to be kind; remember we are enjoined to bear the fruit of the Spirit. The Bible says you, as a man, will and should bear the fruit of the Spirit. We are all called to bear the fruit of the Spirit. This clearly means I no longer live according to the way that the world wants me to live—the worldly definition of what a "real man" ought to be.

My identity is precise when measured by the standard of Christ—not man's rule or standards. I am measured by His standards in being a proper husband.

This calls me to love my wife as Christ loved the Church. Pretty high standard, right—but guess what? You can't do it on your own. He's given you all the tools, the very Spirit of Christ lives in you—submit to His will and He'll do the job!

My job is to let Him be gentle and tender with my wife through me. My job assignment is to wash my wife's feet daily with God's word.

This means I wash her with truth; which means the truth, which is Jesus, as He is the very Word of God. That means I allow Jesus to wash over my wife—continually purifying her with His nature pouring over here, refreshing her daily.

It means that I am to speak to her and with her. *That I am to open my heart, my thoughts, desires to her and to be vulnerable.* When we do these things, it says to her that you are loved, you are accepted, you are amazing. I think the best way that you can be the best friend of your wife is to tell her the truth in love. In James 1:19 it teaches us that we are to be good listeners, slow to answer, to listen, and of course to listen in and genuine effort to understand from where she's coming. It is talking to my wife in the way of a "Rema." Not by an "objective word" but by a "inner speaking" – it's like reading the Bible—yes, but are we "hearing by the Word of Christ" . . . *"Faith comes by hearing and hearing by the Word of Christ"* (Rom. 10:17). On what level are we, as husbands, communicating with our wives—superficially or truly listening, hearing, understanding? Trust me, that's at a wholly different level . . . it's at the level of Christ! When you communicate with your wife on this level, then mutual goals, dreams, you name it, will be fulfilled because then you really are hearing by the Word of Christ.

She has signed up to be with you for the rest of her life. She really does want to know the deepest longings of your heart. If she hears you saying *I'm fine*, she assumes something is wrong with her—she's done something wrong. Be open and talk. You don't want the enemy, whom she's already fighting, to have a position of placing false guilt upon her on top of all of the other things that the enemy is trying to beat down on her. Take the responsibility and open to her—have her pray for you, pray together.

> ➤ **That action will break the heavy yoke.**

Tanya: This is why I'm so thankful God brought you to me, Honey, instead of other men, because . . .

> ➤ **. . . you truly came as Christ to me, to serve me and not to be served (Mathew 20:28)**

This is deep and beautiful, because on the inside of me it makes me become a softer woman to love, to be gentle, understanding, and enables me to give myself in an affectionate way to you, because you treat me so well. I do not have to work so hard because you carry a lot of my burdens— that is why I can give you more.

Do you know what I am saying? Like it's deep, because a lot of women I know used to be very hardhearted—over time they got that way. They wouldn't open up. They just kept everything inside and wouldn't say how they really felt about their relationship with their husbands. The Lord was preparing me for you. He was softening me to depend on Him as my Husband and Lord. Yes, even being my Man; but He did so in the right way. I'm not being prideful here—but neither am I that "independent woman" who doesn't need any man to help her. I saw that Man in you, James—why would I ever be an "independent woman" after seeing Christ in you!

James: Well, I think, as it is with anyone who is hard hearted, self-willed and self-centered . . . they want to take on this role of appearing to others to be so strong and confident. Yet what they are really missing out on, in my assessment, is this: God says He wants to give us a heart of flesh in exchange for our heart of stone (Ezk. 36:26). So, if you really look at the character of Christ in the Bible it continually describes Him moving with compassion (Matt. 14:14) . . .

> *A person who is moved with compassion is already in a place of tenderness, gentleness— a place of surrender.*

Jesus could have said, "Well, what if I just command thousands of angels to come down and smack you all senseless." No way! There are a lot of people with broken hearts. In what way did He understand the brokenness found in so many hearts?

How? He walked in a place of compassion and gentleness from a platform, a foundation of love. If you try to be strong headed, strong willed, then you are all the more chasing after your own plans and worldly dreams, instead of being surrendered to the Lordship of Jesus Christ.

Jesus knew who He was. He never doubted the abilities of His Father. So He's able to walk into every situation and know what to say. He'll never say something like: "Oh man, I don't know what to do I'm so frustrated, stumped, and this has got my heart so depressed," etc. But rather, the competence of Christ walks in and surrenders to the Father by saying, "Father what do you want to do here?" He could say, "*Not my will but thine be done*" (Lu. 22:42) because, listen up, He had the very same will of the Father. Jesus didn't have one will and His Father have another will—they BOTH had the same will. The Father and the Son were in eternal submission and will. Ever wonder why when speaking about how husbands and wives should respond to one another, we first hear this: "*Submitting to one another in the fear of God*" (Eph. 5:21)? Do you think the "one another" just means men, excluding women? I think it has a whole lot to do about the Godhead's eternal submission—and that's the fellowship into which we have been called. Wow! That's a biggie.

> **How should we handle this?"**

His boldness with assertiveness speaks out the very things that need to be said, from a place of love. The things that He said were to build others up—to lift them up, not to elevate Himself. Remember Jesus with this confidence never elevated Himself.

He only elevated the Father. Remember what He said: *"If you have seen me you have seen the Father; I and My Father are one."* (John 10:30) Yes, one in will and one in submission.

A DAD

For me, becoming a dad was one of the best blessings. When I was growing up, I was badly abused by my dad.

I never knew what it was like to be loved, encouraged, or fathered. I was healed by Father God who became my Father role model as He proved to me that a father is loving and is not to be feared, rather, he can be fully trusted.

I am so appreciative that the Lord later in life brought me to the one called Papa. He treated me as a son. Always believing in me as he kept encouraging me into becoming a successful man. I will always be so grateful for Papa's love for me. *He showed me that a real man can be so very gentle and kind.* That' exactly who Papa is, and so much more.

A FRIEND

When I was in high school, I learned the value of friendship and that benefits of being a good friend attracted great friends to me. As friends, we had fun, helped each other with homework, and most definitely horsed around in class and on campus.

We were there for each other, even when some went through the hardest times, and experienced so much heartache at such a young age.

My friends helped me to see a living example of what Jesus is like. In John 15:15 Jesus said that He calls us *friends.* It began to really sink into my heart transforming my way of thinking that the God of the universe and of all creation wants to be my friend. What a profound love.

A SON

Growing up I only knew that I was a son—but just as a definition . . . I never felt like a son. I only knew that everything that I did, no matter how perfect, it was never perfect enough for my dad. I cleaned, and yet would be beaten for water spots on the glasses in the cupboards. If there was a smudge in the glass ashtray, then I would be beaten in the head with that large heavy glass sphere until I nearly passed out.

Getting an A- was horrible, yet when I got all A+s, I was mocked for how I wanted to be better than him . . . yikes! I will never forget, somewhere in my mid-twenties, I was invited to a men's retreat. Upon arrival, I quickly realized that the Lord was probably up to something. The theme of the retreat was dealing with the hurts of a father.

I will never forget—I will always be thankful for what took place that Saturday evening. I went forward for prayer. I sat on the chair and assumed *prayed for position* . . . hands on my knees and palms facing up. It did not take long to realize that the dozen or so other men were all receiving prayer. Then more time passed and still nothing. I placed my face into my hands and buried my face.

Soon after that, a man kneeled before me and wrapped his arms around me; he pulled my head onto his chest and held me tightly. I cried because it was an answer to the prayer that I whispered to God earlier during lunch while all alone *"God, I just wish I knew what it was like to be held by my dad."* I was healed so quickly as I learned that God truly hears my every cry, my every thought.

> ➤ **I realized that a father's affection for his son is so empowering and freeing.**

LORDSHIP: WHO IS YOUR LORD?

It comes down to a question of lordship. It also comes down to the question of stewardship. *What or who is the most important person or thing in your life?* I have noticed over the years that too many men have idols because that is the god they serve. As you can see, this begins to create the issue of why men cannot be who they are supposed to be in Christ Jesus when their heart is divided. As the Bible says, you cannot serve God and mammon. We as men first must choose whom we are going to serve. That is the first step for many.

There is no room for lordship when you are the Lord of your own life. I think a confident woman is a beautiful creation just like a confident man is a beautiful creation. But if it is based upon your pride which says, "I'll prove to others that I'm better than others," then it's from a place of pride in self-righteousness, self-will which has no place for humility and lordship.

PROPER LEADER

Tanya: How are men supposed to be proper leaders?

James: Yes, so in the same way, when you walk into the room, you are to bring life, instruction, words of wisdom from a place of love, *because only that confidence comes from a life being surrendered to the Lordship of Christ.* That is what gives you the ability to walk into an environment, knowing what to do. Never puzzled, never stumped; but, with the ability to have the understanding and to know in what direction how things should be moving.

When we encourage others to partner with us, as opposed to some who want to just show up and take over and put others in their place . . . you know, "You have got to do it my way or the highway" . . . that is just pride and arrogance. I'm not suggesting there's not a time to be a leader—that's a different topic, but **a true leader gets others to partner**

with them, shares a common goal, a common vision, and he gets others to buy into that goal. The most successful leaders, once they can encourage others to see how it will benefit them all, then others will naturally follow the leader.

These results of being a proper leader come from the man following the best leader of all, Jesus Christ—they will want to *imitate* Him. To lead properly, we must have the mindset of serving. Leading is a choice that says, "I will lead by living out a life that role models to others what it should look like." I have never met a genuine, successful leader who was not actively practicing those things in daily life. Remember, Jesus was followed by many people because of what He did; and what He said all aligned into a message of hope. Those following Him were a result of what they saw Him doing, saying, and practicing in His daily life.

Tanya: Right. He includes everyone in on the gameplan like the Lord includes us to be one with him. Honey, that is what I love about you. You are not like a "bossing around" boss who would tell me what, when, where, how and why to speak or do things but you speak to me as a real partner— we're really in this together—with honor and respect. There's not just "input" – there's "output" – there's fellowship! But when I am not treated as an equal then my ideas, output, means nothing. Your spouse must be coachable, approachable and open to you . . . not intimidating.

A lot of people are not this way. They are just stuck in their own ways or bad habits. Many do not want to change or want to hear another person's opinion or heart even to ask for help. It is sad to see the arrogance of people, but I praise the Lord that God is showing us how it is supposed to truly be. I know it's not easy when you return home from a hard day's work to listen as Christ's listens—but by God's grace you do. Same goes for me when I'm exhausted from a day running all over the place—yet, God's grace allows me to listen to you. What an amazement it is to hear the Word of Christ in one another and to listen as He listens.

I am so thankful for you as a man of God because, I had that relationship with the Lord before you came into my life. I grew to know that Jesus was kind, gentle, tender, loving—always embracing me and hugging me, holding me. That is how I see Jesus. I know He is a King and the Master and Lord of Lords—yet He is all-embracing and so loving.

This intimate, beautiful way Christ expresses Himself to me is so very precious—this truly moves my heart. The Lord treats me like a queen. That's *why I'm so thankful for you because you treat me very similar to the way Christ treats me.* That is why I called you at one time *Lord* because the way you treat me (1 Pet. 3:6; Eph. 5:33), the way you honor me, it's like . . . it's easy to respect you back . . . because you give me so much love and affection—it's all that I need.

With my ex, I never got that. That is what made it so hard to respect and honor him—someone who treated me so horribly. It is so easy with you; it is the extreme opposite. A woman always needs a man who's gentle, loving, and kind—like Jesus. And, by the way, that's what a guy needs in a woman. He wants a woman who is gentle and kind and loving too. It is both of us having the same image and godly nature of Christ—it goes for both of us.

OVERCOMING ADDICTION

James: In the book of Titus, especially in Chapter 3, it describes the guidelines of how we should conduct ourselves as a follower of Jesus. Although some of the more modern forms of sinning are not precisely mentioned, we can certainly and should absolutely keep ourselves from all types of sexual sins. Under *conquerseries.com* we read:

> ➤ **Mind-Blowing Statistics about Pornography**

. . . and The Church states:

"... it is no secret that men inside the church are just as addicted to porn as those who are outside of the church. Statistically about 65 percent of all men, even those who are professing Christians, view pornography online at least once per month. Porn increases the odds of marital unfaithfulness [by] more than 300 percent. Around 56% of divorcees said that because one of the spouses were addicted to porn . . . it influenced the reason to divorce."

This ought not to be. When we engage in any type of perversion or sexual sin, we drag our Savior through the mud.

The Holy Spirit sees it all and cries out for us to choose to accept His help to overcome those addictions and destructive behaviors. The great news is: He can help us have complete victory in all things . . . to completely overcome all strongholds. You can be one with your wife! What we do affects our wife as well. The same spirit that dwells in you dwells in her also, because you are one in Christ. You cannot throw a rock into a pond of water and think that it will not create ripples or not influence anything else. As a follower of Jesus, you are crucified with Christ and it is no longer I who lives but Christ lives in me (Galatians 2:20). We are called to no longer live by the flesh, but by the Spirit.

One of the greatest reasons to read, pray, and seek the Lord daily is so that we do not give any place to the enemy. If you are giving part of your heart and affection to someone other than your wife, then you are not loving your wife as Christ loves the Church. *A divided heart cannot stand strong against the enemy when you welcome him openly into your marriage* (Matt. 12:25-NIV). The solution is to fully surrender to the Lordship of Jesus. Remember, every yoke and bondage can be broken in the name of Jesus (Gal. 5:1).

As men we are to lead our family from wherever they are into a place of holiness. We must consider the impact that we have on our children. Do we really want our legacy to include addictions to such destructive behaviors? If not, then we must be willing to become vulnerable and honest in seeking help from mature believers. The sad truth is only around 7% of churches have resources in place to help men with this kind of addiction. We need to change that. Will you be the one to change it?

> **Will you answer the call of the Lord and say, "Send Me"? (Isa. 6:8)**

For many years I served with a scouting group called Royal Rangers. I had the privilege of working with so many honorable men that were committed to excellence before the Lord. We had around 70 boys from 3rd grade through high school. One of the things that I observed is that these boys looked at us all the time. How did we treat them? What type of language did we use? Were our conversations wholesome? Did we ever talk poorly about others? As men, we need to always step up and obey that Word of the Lord and see to it that everything we do and say represents the Lord as well as possible. This next generation is counting on us. They desperately need us to walk out our lives as followers of Jesus in an honorable way that glorifies the Lord.

WHY MEN NEED TO TAKE THEIR PROPER PLACE

As men we need to rise up and take our rightful place. It is sad and troubling to my heart when I see that it is mostly women who run the church; Sunday school teachers, working the help tables, setting up the food services, and so on. *Remember, we are to live out a life of service.* **How can our wives submit to us if we are not willing to submit to the Lord or the pastor of our own church or, frankly, to one another?**

I have been going to a men's group of late. One of the things that I appreciate so much is that these 300 men are sold out for Jesus Christ. The sad truth is that is a rare thing. We have got to get into the habit of turning off the TV, leaving the sporting events for another time, and committing ourselves to the Lord. This specific season now upon us warrants us to stop playing games with God while living out a life as Titus states we should live. We, as men do need to hang out together and have fellowship with one another. But let us keep it glorifying to God and edifying to one another as we have fun in the things of the Lord. We should live a life where our very character makes it obvious to all who see us that our identity is in Jesus—that's how real men live out their lives.

Please, do not misunderstand me. There is a time and place for watching football—those types of pleasures. But as for me, right now because of this season we are in a state and a country demanding we need to set those things aside and focus on the kingdom—this "place" has entered into the hands of the "Lawless One." I truly am a son of the living God. The Holy Spirit lives in me. That makes me His property—representing the kingdom of heaven. Therefore, my very body is the temple of the Holy Spirit, the Lord of host, the King of Kings. I win in the name of Jesus. There is no condemnation as Jesus fully paid the price to purchase me. He has fully forgiven me. It is because of His blood shed on that bloody cross which has freed me from any and all sin, the fear death, and the devil. *"So if the Son sets you free, you shall be free indeed"* (John 8:36). So, in Jesus' name, you're free . . . In Jesus Name, we rebuke you, Satan . . . my old man is dead . . . I'm free indeed!

Focus on declaring your identity—who you really are in Christ, in the One New Man. Declare the truth of who you are!

SECTION THREE: HEALING

". . . For I am the Lord Who heals you."

(Exodus. 15:26)

Chapter 6
The Healing Hand of The Lord

The Lord wants to save and heal you and your marriage. We can say that it is best for God's healing to take place, even before you get married. It is especially important because you do not want to bring the baggage of your past into a marriage. However, sometimes the Lord will teach us, after we're married, that we can become a healing balm to each other no matter what past has not been healed.

WHAT IS YOUR FOUNDATION?

Tanya: At the beginning I knew God revealed this matter of healing to us; however, it is better to have that inner healing of your heart prior to marriage—to allow the Holy Spirit to truly heal you from all your past hurts. I know it takes time to experience complete healing; however, again, when you do come into a covenant relationship with your spouse, you should have already dealt with the most serious things of your past. You do not want to bring those major hurts into the marriage. Honey, can you share with us a little on what I've just said here?

James: Briefly, until we have the core issues in our heart and our mind—even our emotions and will—genuinely healed we'll still be operating from a different foundation, a fractured mindset . . .it simply is not the best one. What I'm saying here is that when one is not fully surrendered to the lordship of Jesus—as I have shared throughout this text—one is really on shaky ground because you're building upon two foundations which are contrary to one another.

> ➤ **There is a foundation of love and a foundation of fear.**

As we begin to operate in our new nature, which is a foundation of love, it begins to deal with the nature of fear into

87

which we were born.   Recognizing that our "old man" has

been dealt with by His cross (Rom. 6:6) . . .

"Knowing this, that our old man is crucified with him, that the body of sin might be destroyed, that henceforth we should not serve sin."

That is the starting place where we begin to allow the healing hand of the Lord. It is in those places in our lives in order to begin   the renewing,   the transformation of our hearts and minds—*knowing this*. It is what is in our hearts, how we have perceived things and have interpreted them through the lens of our old man who kept hidden all those hurtful things. Listen, it's a process which continues throughout our walk with the Lord.

Tanya: I believe a lot of men and women need a great deal of inner healing. I think that is where it really begins because when we are inadequately raised or have mentally, even physically, been deeply hurt, we do not know how to properly love.   It's difficult for us with such baggage to discern the truth. What is the right thing to do and how to live? Too often if we do not allow His inner healing to take place, then we follow the inherited traits given to us by our parents, because that was the main model or example we observed—whether we want to admit it or not.

It takes a lot of investment in time for inner healing . . . a lot of deliverance, a lot of change of the mindset, especially in your identity. So much needs to be adjusted to the "mind of Christ" (1 Cor. 2:16). *The main goal for a man and a woman* is to really change and be transformed into the image of Christ—from glory to glory—because that is what God designed us to be from the beginning. Adam and Eve were to have that oneness and unity in love with each other and with the Almighty:

> "Now the Lord is the Spirit; and where the Spirit of the Lord is, there is liberty. But we all, with unveiled face, beholding as in a mirror the glory of the Lord, **are being transformed** into the same image from glory to glory, just as by the Spirit of the Lord" (2 Cor. 3:17-18 NKJV)

Honey, isn't it so—the more we behold the beauty of the Lord Jesus, the more we are transformed into what we behold? We're like a mirror turned to the Lord—when you look at the mirror you see what the mirror is beholding . . . we, the mirror, reflect the glory of the Lord more and more!

Inner healing, lasting healing, can only take place when that hurt is exposed in the presence of the Lord . . . only when we turn our mirror to behold Him, then, and then only, are we being transformed.

CHOOSING TO LOVE

That is really the biggest value, meaning, and purpose of life is to know the love of God, to love ourselves and love others properly. I believe, the main purpose and destiny why we are here is to learn how to love, to walk in unity with Christ, as one, demonstrating His love as a role model to others.

I'm so overwhelmed that He gave us His New Commandment that we are to love one another only as Jesus has loved us—we are enabled to love one another by Jesus Who has loved us!

> "A New Commandment I give you: Love one another as I have loved you, so you also must love one another. By this everyone will know that you are My disciples, if you love one another" (John 13:34-35—Berean Study Bible)

When we go into the presence of Jesus with our new bodies, our glorified bodies, He'll ask us if we kept His New Commandment—O Lord, may it be so!

I remember in the middle of the night I was so hurt by my immediate family. I heard the Lord speaking to my heart, *"Do you love them?"* That was so profound. It was extremely hard for me because of the deep and lasting wound from the pain they had caused within me for such a long time. It was that bitterness and unforgiveness in my heart that I had to let go.

It took some time to think, to ponder it. I prayed and asked the Holy Spirit to help me to love them, because I knew I couldn't do it on my own strength. I chose to love them no matter what, which allowed me to love them with an honest genuine love, I said, *"Yes Lord I do love them."* Then the peace came over me because His love flowed through me to them and then I was able to sleep and rest in His embrace.

The next morning, I was in Father God's presence as a little girl. I deeply experienced and sensed the nature of His pure love. I knew that moment that I was His little child and that I loved my Father God. I came to grasp how His love was able to overflow to my daughters and to everyone else—so great is the love of Christ! I pray that you will know and connect with your Maker, your Heavenly Father and experience His unconditional love for you.

James: You are so right, my love. I am so thankful to the Lord for the healing that you allowed the Lord to do in your heart . . . you continually allow His love to take place. *We need to all understand that our healing and deliverance is a process.*

For some people, it is an instant miracle. More often it is a journey that not only heals us but reveals to us the deep nature of the Lord. The Lord desires us to know Him in deep intimacy as our Deliverer, the One Who heals us. It is about learning to trust Him and to know He wants the best for us. One of His Names in Hebrew is "Jehovah Rapha"—*"O Lord my God, I cried out to You, and You healed me"* (Psa. 30:2 NKJV)

Sometimes in this fallen world it is difficult to see or understand how anyone has pure and great intentions for us; someone who just wants to *lavish* love and goodness upon us. Yet, that is exactly what the Lord desires for us (Ephesians 1:8). Part of this chapter just reminds us that God has chosen us and has cleansed us through Jesus. This gives us the *hope* that we need to know that God wants us to be complete, a whole person inside.

In 2 Corinthians 3:17 we have the promise of Freedom, because if you have been born again, and the Holy Spirit lives in you, then this is where the Spirit of the Lord is, so you have Freedom! When we are "joined to the Lord"—in His sweet fellowship—then, as it says, we are One Spirit . . . our spirit is in complete fellowship with His Spirit:

"But he who is joined to the Lord becomes one spirit with Him" (1 Cor. 6:17).

CHOOSE TO FORGIVE

One of the beginning places to this freedom, after you have accepted Jesus as your Lord and Savior, comes when you forgive those who hurt you. We get a glimpse into that in Ephesians 4:32 which says:

"Be kind to one another, tenderhearted, forgiving one another as God in Christ forgave you."

When I read this, it was the beginning of getting my heart and mind properly aligned with the Word of God. The good news is all things are possible in Christ Jesus (Luke 1:37 and Matthew 19:26).

Tanya: I love these verses; they have spoken so deeply into my heart—to know that the truth has set me free. Now I want to forgive . . . I want to love others as Christ has loved and forgiven me . . . He has changed my heart and mind.

James: These verses begin to lay the foundation for true healing. There are many similar verses, that the Lord wants us to know that He is able and wants to heal us. *Forgiving others in my experience is when I begin to see others the way that Jesus sees them.* Well, how does He see them?

The same way He sees me and you. He sees you as someone whom He wants to lavish His love, grace, and forgiveness upon. When we exercise the act of forgiving someone, we are allowing the very nature of God to flow through us and we are representing God in one of His greatest character traits.

At one point I truly had to repent because it was my own behavior that caused others to hurt me. There were times in my past when I would posture myself as being arrogant—"the-I-am-always-right"—attitude.

Why was that the case? Well, when I was growing up, I found my place of escape and comfort from the abuse I suffered by absorbing as much knowledge as possible.

It was awesome to become a genius, but it was at the expense of hurting others. Unfortunately, I carried this for many years into my adulthood. Alas! I was exposed, and I knew that I wanted to love others just for who they were—just like how Jesus loves me for exactly how He created me . . . still I was a hurting man.

> ➢ **What was the cure? It was repentance.**

As real prayer began to work in my life and as I began to believe that God Himself really wanted to pour out His love in my life, and that His very nature in me could conquer all my inefficiencies—it was then I was able to let Him complete His work in me by putting my trust in His sufficiency.

It was a huge step of faith because my view of a father was that of a violent man who only sought me out to physically and emotionally damage me.

TESTIMONY OF GOD'S HEALING HAND

Tanya: First of all I want to share this testimony of God's healing hand upon me. When I was 16 years old, I was working on my first job at a thrift store. I hurt my back as I was lifting the clothes off the rack. This injury sent me off to the chiropractor—my disc was completely dislocated. There were times when I was in so much pain that I could not move. It affected me so much that I had to lay in bed for prolonged periods of time.

I was praying to Jesus to heal me and to show me a miracle. Before that accident happened, I was reading in the Bible in Mark 5:25-34 about the lady who touched Jesus' garment to be healed from a blood issue. I believed in my heart . . . I wanted to see that take place in my own body. Then it happened to me!

It was very similar to her story in the sense that as she tried to get help from so many doctors, she still could not get healed. Different chiropractors came to help me and made me worse off than before—just like the lady who suffered with the blood issue.

Gradually, my condition worsened. The pain was excruciating. There were times when I was driving in the car where my feet, then my legs, would be completely paralyzed. I couldn't move them; I would say and pray for healing through the blood of Jesus—then they would start to work again. Once again I could go back to driving safely—God protected me in those moments . . . praise God!

Notwithstanding, I still was in such pain just sitting in church . . . there were a lot of things I simply could no longer do. I couldn't even pick up a gallon of milk; that's how intense the pain had become. Here I was, this young person, overwhelmed with pain . . . I remember when I went to church, and had the people pray for my healing. I was expecting that in my heart and mind it would come true as soon as they had finished praying for me. I believed that I was healed.

I went home, and I told my mom that by faith I was healed—even though the pain persisted. I declared with faith, believing I was healed—then, right at that very moment when I told my mom, I literally felt a click in my back! Everything completely went back to normal; everything is healed in Jesus' name, praise God.

The next morning I awoke—it was like I was born again like a little baby. Praise the Lord! God did a huge miracle for me. He heard my prayer, the cry of my heart, and He healed me in His perfect timing and plan.

Then about a month later I was under attack—the pain resurfaced . . . but this time it was twice as painful. I remember I declared: *Devil, get behind me Satan.* I had a strong conviction that I was to rebuke the Devil plaguing me with this sickness. I had to take my healing back knowing that God truly did heal me. All doubt was banished—again, the pain completely left me ushering in incessant praise to God.

Now I am healed and whole! Moreover, He has given me two beautiful little girls to the praise of His Name. I believe this for you as you are praying for your healing. Believe God's timing is perfect for you to declare your healing. Yes, believe, trust, and put your hope steadfastly in the Lord Jesus Christ and His Word. Stand upon the Word of God right now to usher in your healing in fullness—meeting all your needs. Let the Lord heal you and strengthen you. I pray that through my testimony you will have greater faith to believe . . . just to trust Him with child-like faith. For He can do it for you as He did it for me. Blessings.

Tanya: Honey, I am so thankful to the Lord for you and your life here on earth. God has surely protected our lives from so many injuries, trials—even cancer (both of us). Tell our readers your amazing story about God's deep healing hand in your life?

James: Yes, another healing was needed for me—it was physical. On August 31st of 1996 I was rear-ended in the company truck. I was doing about 15 miles per hour when a truck hit me doing around 55-60 miles per hour. My neck was broken. My left shoulder was torn and my back was messed up. I was knocked unconscious. When I was at the hospital, I was told about all my injuries . . . that is when I began my 11-year journey to get well. Being the devout Christian which I truly believe I was, I demanded that God had to heal me because that is what His Word says—surely, You are not a God Who lies (Hebrews 6:18)?

Well, that was just the beginning of my journey. There's no doubt in my mind God has every ability to heal my body and that healing is easy for Him. After all, He created me! *But the real issue was the condition of my heart, my attitude . . . I was in desperate need . . . I really needed to become a loving person delivered from the hurts from my past.* God used this season to heal my heart. The physical healing came through many years of having surgeries, physical therapy, and many procedures to finally get me as physically well as possible.

Thankfully, I am physically functional and able to do many things which I normally could do before the accident. Trust me; I really did want to be supernaturally healed. I am grateful for everyone who prayed for me. But looking back, I am so thankful that my Lord knew what was best for me and healed my heart and set me free during this physical time of healing. Sometimes I think that we all question God's plan, His wisdom, His will, and His ways. I was physically damaged so that He could inwardly heal me—Oh, the wisdom of the Lord!

> ➤ **But I have decided to make Jesus the Lord of my life.**

During this time I surrendered my life to Him. I declared as Jesus did: Not my will be done, but Thine be done . . . let me fulfill the will of my Heavenly Father.

During this time is when I realized as never before the ministry of Holy Spirit. He became my Comforter, my Teacher, the source of my true identity. It was so necessary for me to learn all that I am comes from the Lord. No matter what I think, how I feel, or how much effort I put into trying to make something happen—nothing of eternal value happens until the Holy Spirit makes it so.

Tanya: As we are writing this chapter, the Holy Spirit woke us both up today at 3:33 a.m. to spend time alone with Him. He has taught us to go to Him first and talk about everything before going to one another and talking about it. This was a huge lesson for us and it can be for many marriages. We are to seek and talk to the Lord first before going to our spouses.

Our spouses will never be perfect. Surely, Honey, you are not, and neither am I. I like reading *Crosswalk Couples Devotional* about "What to do with a Broken Heart" by Lynette Kittle . . . as she explains:

". . . if our focus has been on our spouse to behave perfectly, to meet all our needs and to complete us, we will be left disappointed. But we can put those expectations on God, Who will never fail us. What expectations do you need to take off of your spouse and give over to God? What hurts do you need to give to Christ? What would it look like for you to extend forgiveness to your spouse today?"

I had to let go of my own expectations for my husband and put it on God. Only Jesus can make me happy and completely satisfy me. We are both a work in progress for the Holy Spirit to do His deep work inside of us to change and heal us from our past and present situations. He is my Friend to Whom I talk with about everything. In Proverbs 17:17 it says:

"A friend loves at all times, and a brother is born for a time of adversity."

We are friends with God and with each other by talking first to God and then loving each other enough to talk through everything with each other. It's so amazing to experience how the Holy Spirit really cares about our needs and concerns inside of our hearts, minds, and circumstances. He wanted to hear me tell Him everything by giving it to Him . . . giving to Him all that is going in my life. God said, *"I Am the One that heals and knows it all. Ask, Seek and Knock in Mathew 7:7.* It is a prayer of perseverance to keep on asking until you are given and receiving by seeking His face to find Him and His mercy until our needs are truly met . . . to keep on knocking and believing that the doors will be opened. I am so thankful to know that Holy Spirit knows me—all of us, all our heart issues, all our hurting pain—He understands it all. His Word says that He is "touched by the feeling of our infirmities" (Heb. 4:15). Isn't it time to come and spend time alone with the Holy Spirit—Who ever intercedes on our behalf—to tell Him everything inside of our heart, your heart, to heal you? Yes, He knows already—but He longs to hear you tell Him, to speak to Him . . . and in that fellowship, His healing will begin to do its perfect work.

It is amazing after we have talked and processed our issues before one another that we begin to understand each other—we're able to draw closer in relationship which is deeper, more intimate and enriching. Talking things through is a healing way of not allowing the enemy and the hurt to surface. Being honestly open to one another about our good and bad experiences is so important in our marriage.

Remember, pray first with God. Tell Him everything, then go and share with your spouse by opening your heart. Then see what the Lord will do in your marriage . . . how He will draw you both closer in deepening your relationship. My prayer, our prayer, is to ask the Lord what He wants to share with you; He said:

> ➤ *"Tell them that I came to save them and heal them inside and out."* **(Jeremiah 17:14)**

Yes! He has come to save your marriage and to heal your hearts to be fully whole inside and out. In our next chapter we will be talking about the process of deeper inner healing for your spirit, heart, soul, mind, and body—complete healing!

Chapter 7
The Inner Healing of your Heart, Soul, Mind, Spirit and Body

This is certainly the most meaningful topic for anyone's life. Why? Because it has to do with who you are, the actual essence of a person. It is all about how we think. The Bible says—and we have come to fully experience and believe it to be true—in Proverbs 23:7: *"For as you think, you are."* We're going to challenge you and ourselves right now. Go ahead and do something, anything at all right now, you choose what you are to do for the next 15 seconds.

One thing we can assure you is that no matter what you chose to do or not to do, you had to think about it and give thought to the topic that we just mentioned. Our minds are in control. Our bodies, unless there is a medical condition, just do not do all on their own. They just don't hop into action without a thought that preceded the action that takes place.

OUR MIND

Tanya: Honey, how do we get our mind to function properly the way God has designed it to be?

James: We are in charge of our own thoughts. God gave us the ability to function with self-control with the help of Holy Spirit (Galatians 5:23). Thankfully, we have the Holy

Spirit to give us the ministering ability to receive the necessary ability to be transformed in our minds (Romans 12:2). One of my observations over the years is seeing people make excuses of saying things like: "I cannot help it; it is just who I am." In other words a confession that "I'm out of control!"

Allow me to introduce you to 2 Corinthians 10:5 which in part says that: "*We take captive every thought to* **make it** *obedient to Christ.*" Notice the word "*make it.*" So, we have the God-given ability to take charge of our thoughts and make our thoughts surrender to the Lordship of Jesus Christ—we are NOT robots. This is the very ministry and purpose, the function of His Holy Spirit; the supernatural habitation of the Holy Spirit in us to transform us into the image of Christ from within.

Tanya: I like looking and reading many Scriptures around our home to keep our mind set on God.

James: Yes, we have scriptures posted throughout our home. One of my favorites is Philippians 4:8 which says:

"Finally brethren, whatever is true, whatever is honorable, whatever is just, whatever is pure, whatever is lovely, whatever is commendable, if there is any excellence, if there is anything worthy of praise, think about these things."

I know that sometimes it is difficult to know what we are to think about; therefore, I am thankful to the Lord that He even tells us what to think on so that we do not fall into thoughts or situations that could possibly harm us in some way.

Our thoughts are either going to make us or break us. Too often people focus on trying to get rid of bad thoughts. If they are angry for example, most of the time they are encouraged to focus on getting rid of their anger. I personally question that technique. Why? Because in Isaiah 61:3 it says that the Lord "*gives us beauty instead of ashes.*" Throughout the Bible it always stresses exchanging things with us. He gave us a new nature instead of the old one (2 Corinthians 5:17).

Why do I focus so much on our mind and how we think? Because we are no longer our own if we have accepted Christ as our Savior and Lord (Galatians 2:20). Our body is the temple of the Holy Spirit as stated in 1 Corinthians 6:19-20. Our bodies were designed to give us great joy knowing that the Lord is absolutely committed to our success during His sanctification work in us. This process is part of a lifelong journey, but we can have joy knowing that He has amazing plans for our life (Jeremiah 29:11).

We can trust the Lord and count on His faithfulness. The Lord is absolutely sure of His own abilities to bring forth the changes that He so desires to see in us for our mutual benefit.

The benefit to us is that we can walk in the full confidence of Christ Jesus knowing fully that we are accepted in the Beloved; therefore, we have every reason to rise up and celebrate each moment of every day.

Tanya: There are many benefits to keep our mind set on the Lord.

James: Yes, the next benefit is recognizing that a mind that is set on the Lord brings out what Romans 8:6 says:

"For the mind set on the flesh is death, but the mind set on the Spirit is life and peace."

Most people I have met in life are to some degree looking for peace. Even some Christians I know seek out their peace by resorting to the use of drugs, alcohol, porn, and many other things of the flesh that can harm them.

However, when we focus on allowing the Holy Spirit to work in our hearts and minds, we then can begin the truest and most satisfying form of peace which is godly peace—peace that is attached to Life, not destruction.

OUR SOUL

Tanya: The soul is our mind, will, and emotions. It is so important to get our soul healed up and aligned with God's Spirit. Our soul affects our body 99%. Getting our soul healed by the power of the Holy Spirit is so powerful. So-called "psychosomatic" conditions can have horrendous negative results on our bodies—but these harmful conditions experienced in our bodies are derived from our souls. Yes, "It's all in your mind"—true, but it's more than real in your body!

James: All these activities which involve our mind affect our whole soul and the health of it. Our soul's health is typically a byproduct of the healthy condition of our mind. My soul is greatly influenced by the verse: *"There is therefore now no condemnation for those in Christ Jesus"* (Romans 8:1). My soul, and probably your soul, needs to know that because of God's great mercy, we have escaped the judgment that we deserved, and by His grace we stand without being condemned before the Lord.

> ➢ **I believe that one of our deepest soul needs is to know that God has not given up on us.**

We're never too far gone as long as breath is in us. Have we committed too much sin to the extent that God has chosen to finally given up on us? The truth is God sees us as righteous in Christ Jesus, without any blemish or stain of sin—that is our ultimate potential in God's sight. Remember, Jesus said on the cross: *"It is finished!"* We cannot be in a state of confusion here. Either Jesus is exactly Who He said He is and who He said we are: We are completely washed, forgiven, and have eternal life, or it's just all a lie. The truth is the Truth. *O, how we struggle with God's goodness . . . why is it so hard to receive perfect love from a perfect God Who sees us through the lens of Jesus who makes us perfect in the sight of the Father? It's His righteousness; it's His blood which cleanses us of all our sin!*

OUR PHYSICAL BODY

Tanya: Our body's healthy condition is directly affected from our soul—it's about what and how we think.

James: In Proverbs 17:22 it says, *"A happy heart makes good like a medicine."* How is our heart made happy? It is the result of a *mind staying focused on the Spirit.* The rest of that same verse says, *"A broken spirit dries up the bones."* We certainly have heard that much of our body's health is directly connected to what is happening in our heart, in our mind. One of the most important influencers of having a healthy body is how we think.

However, the counterpart of that is taking responsibility to live a responsible life by caring for this temple that the Lord has allowed us to use. One of the last things that I do not want to see happen is for my health to fail thereby cheating my family out of enjoying life to the fullest together. By simply refusing to bring my body under the Lordship of Jesus I cheat my family. If something should happen to my health, then I can live with the outcome knowing that I did my part to be a man who lived a self-controlled life and was the best steward that I could be for my physical body—God knows!

I want my life to be that living example to my family of what a man of the Lord should look like when he is fully surrendered to the lordship of Jesus Christ. *One of my goals is to leave a legacy where our children and grandchildren will see the goodness of God in my life, by seeing it in my actions.* It is only then that my words will have the most impactful value because my actions will always speak much louder then my words will ever speak. Don't look at what I say—look at my deeds which will always speak louder than my words. Words can be cheap—may, by God's grace, my actions keep speaking beyond any words I may have spoken.

Tanya: I pray over myself and my family that: *"Through Jesus' stripes you are healed"* (Isaiah 53:5). *I bind this spirit of infirmity and loosen a spirit of life and healing* (Luke

103

13:10-17). *I pray that your body is recognized as the temple of the Holy Spirit and that no sickness or disease belong there* (1 Cor. 6:19-20). This is a powerful prayer that I pray over myself and others. It releases them from pain and stress in their body when it's prayed in faith. You must ask, declare, and believe to receive healing—it will, can, and shall be done (Matthew 21:22).

SPRIT AND SOUL AND BODY AS A WHOLE

Tanya: Our spirit man is healed, whole, and complete as one with the Holy Spirit, when we accept the Lord Jesus Christ into our hearts. One of my reflections over the years is seeing people when they get that healing process with the Lord in all these areas—then they become whole. God wants us to be like it's written:

> *"May God himself, the God of peace, sanctify you through and through. May your whole spirit and soul and body be kept blameless at the coming of our Lord Jesus Christ"* (1 Thessalonians 5:23).

The Lord wants us to be purified Church to be His Bride prepared for His coming. The healing and purifying process is needed whereby we allow His Spirit to take over our souls, hearts, and minds as His Bride, the Church of the Living God. The battle is for our soul, our spirit is joined with His Spirit to transform our soul in order to fight against our flesh within this "body of death." Let us allow the Spirit within our human spirit to penetrate our "soul-life" and subdue our body until we are whole: spirit and soul and body. That is the complete process in marriage—we are becoming more whole . . . being transformed into the very image of Jesus Christ. Honey, what would you like to say about this?

James: Sweetheart, it just proves to me how correct the Bible is and how true it is as it says in Proverbs 23:7, *"For as he thinks in his heart, so is he."* As a person thinks so you are. I always look at how important your mindset is. It is your thoughts that will either make you or break you. Whenever

104

you take on the mind of Christ and allow the Lord to heal those deep inner places, you will be whole—your whole being is affected: spirit and soul and body.

OUR HEARTS

Tanya: God cares about our heart condition more than anything else. He wants our hearts to be healed and whole and connected to Father God, Jesus Christ, and the Holy Spirit as one.

> ➢ **God is after our heart.**

James: The Bible says the issues of life flow out from the heart. It can either be rivers of living water or you can speak things that are not so loving (Proverb 4:23). How important it is to have Christ heal our hearts and minds so out of what Jesus said, our innermost being, will flow out rivers of living water (John 7:38). How desperately we need to speak life, His Life, into so many "death situations." Let us confess life by these living words:

"Death and life are in the power of the tongue, and those who love it will eat its fruit" (Proverbs 18:21).

Tanya: I have noticed through my journey of healing that when I have allowed the Holy Spirit to work and heal my heart, then my soul was made whole. It affected my body by strengthening it, causing my body to be healthy. When I get upset or emotionally frustrated, I get so tired in the day. It's because I allowed negative thoughts or the lies of the enemy or negative circumstances to control my inner life. My spirit is quenched, my soul is downcast, and my body is weakened. It is all three connected as one. We need to allow and ask the Holy Spirit to heal us and to rule and reign in our minds and our hearts.

THE PROCESS OF HEALING

Healing is an ongoing process. Where you ask and allow the Holy Spirit to heal you. If you have deep trauma and wounds it is good to go to be with the people of God, get a Christian counselor or an inner healing class. Reach out, find a person you can pray with who is able to walk through past issues with you. I have learned that depression is anger internally bound up inside a person. Such abandonment and rejection lead to fear and unforgiveness—even bitterness.

> **Forgive yourself and others—it releases you from prison into peace and true freedom only found in God—"let the peace of God referee in your heart" (Col. 3:15).**

You can write down the things which hurt you. Then pray and ask the Holy Spirit to come and show you the truth and to heal you. Every time it is different—so, go with the flow and just be open to Holy Spirit's leading. This way you are truly desiring to walk in His Light—let Him expose those areas in your life. You may know of some—but He knows everything about you! Here's the "cycle of Life" . . .

"If we walk in the light, as He is in the Light, we have fellowship one with another, and the blood of Jesus Christ, His Son, keeps on cleansing us from all sin . . . If we confess our sin, He is faithful and just to forgive us our sin and to cleans us from all unrighteousness" (1 John 1:7, 9).

We long for true fellowship with one another, with our spouses, but we must be willing to "walk in the Light, as He is in the Light." Once we do that, and continue to have that as a lasting "life-style" – then "spots" will show up because His Light will expose them. But praise God, that's why we have the blood of Jesus. Then we confess our sin (spots), and He keeps on cleansing us from all unrighteousness by His precious blood—then the fellowship is restored and the process continues all over again. It is His Light which always exposes but continually keeps on cleansing us from all sin. What a wondrous "cycle of Life!"

I have gone through many places to get true and lasting inner healing. It was amazing to learn and to acknowledge it was God Who was always with me—it was and is always the work of Jesus and the Holy Spirit healing my heart and body and making me whole from the inside—not even the best human therapy could do that. Read Psalm 139 . . . it is such a powerful word to read. It explains that it is always God Who is with you—He alone knows all our days and loves us so much!

I started my healing with *heartchange.org*—it's such an incredibly good program. They have many different workshops and they can be found in many states. They do workshops for individuals, spouses, kids, training on how to know the Holy Spirit, and so much more. Check them out and experience the heart of God, gain freedom, and abundant life. But always remember: It is always the work of the Holy Spirit in your spirit alone Who can transform your soul and conform it to the Image of Christ. Yes, the day will come when you receive your glorified body—then your whole spirit and soul and body "*. . . will be preserved blameless at the coming of our Lord Jesus Christ . . . He who calls you is faithful, who also will do it*" (1 Thess. 5:23-24).

Tanya: Honey, what is the process that you have taken to be healed?

James: This goes back, once again, to His lordship over our lives. *I had to make a choice, a conscious decision to open my heart to the ministry of the Holy Spirit.* Some of the actionable things that I put into place were to daily get into the Bible; to pray during that time when Holy Spirit would be my Teacher—the One Who alone can transform me through the "*washing of water by His Word.*" I realized that it takes the Lord to transform me, because James' transformation power (my works) is what got me into one mess after another back in the day.

I listened to great Christian teachers who spoke specifically on inner healing—how to replace the old by learning to walk in my new nature, the personhood of Jesus. I met with a pastor once a week for months who listened to me, prayed with me, and spoke truth and God's Word into me. I counseled with a phycologist as part of my healing as well. The wounds in my heart and mind were deep, and there were many of them.

Most of all I had to choose to cooperate with the Lord and let Him become Lord in all areas of my life by trusting Him for a better me. Really, I chose to "walk in the light" with trusted brethren who knew that as my "spots" were exposed, the "blood of Jesus" was able to cleanse me of all my sin. Yes, I confessed, but I had His precious blood to keep on cleansing me. Listen, that's why we have the Body of Christ. Oh to learn to walk in fellowship with one another in His Light—His healing Light which always points to the blood of Jesus!

STEPS TO TAKE

The steps on *How to Hold on to Your inner Healing*, by Kristine Dohner, includes sections on:

"Who is God? - The Four Filters - The Truth of Your Identity - Declaring the Truth of Who you Are - and The Importance of Forgiveness."

We have spoken about some of these matters in previous chapters of our text concerning our true identity, and *declaring by using Scriptures which say who we really are in Christ Jesus*. Actually, you can google these Scriptures— read them out loud for they speak of your true identity in Christ.

First and foremost, you need to know Who God is: God is Love as found in 1 John 4:16-19 and John 3:16. Most of us know the verse: *"For God so loved the world that He gave His only begotten son that whosoever believes in Him will not perish, but have eternal life."* God is good, kind, and merciful. He is also altogether the Righteous Judge. He wants to have a personal relationship with you; with all His creation, His family.

It is not a religious tradition full of rules and regulations, but a love story—our relationship with God. We hope that this book has brought you to a greater, fuller understanding of how much God genuinely loves you and wants you to know Him—how much He longs to have a personal relationship with you. This is our foremost expectation on your behalf—for you to know your Maker in all His fullness.

Kristine Dohner explains it this way in: *"The Four Filters, to filter all of our thoughts through"* . . .

1. Jesus Loves Me by His . . .

2. Grace, Love, and Mercy—Everything emanating from the throne of God is wrapped in Grace, Love, and Mercy; therefore, He always talks to us nicely . . . in that . . .

3. Jesus is our advocate (John 17) and . . .

4. The Fruit of the Spirit found in Gal 5:22.

FORGIVENESS AND REPENTANCE

Without repenting of your sins before God and others, and choosing to forgive—your freedom and growth in the Lord may be stifled. It is a choice you make when you forgive others. First it sets you free and others around you. It affects your mental and physical health in a harmful way if you cannot "release" others—otherwise, you will not be released.

Kristine Dohner explains:

"Forgiveness is the BEST gift you can give yourself . . . and those you love. Forgiving those who have wronged you is one of the biggest ways to release blessing and freedom in your own life and free you heart to fully love. The whole point of forgiveness is not to justify wrongs done to us, but rather to let your heart out of prison. It does not mean you must deny your hurt or anger. Now I will be vulnerable, or I will have to trust again. Forgiveness is a choice you make of your own free will—the Greek definition of the word is *paphiemi*: to remit a punishment or cancel a debt. Letting

109

go of your resentment and bitterness of the other person—
this is a great way to get you out of prison."

> **I had to choose to forgive, release, and bless
that person** . . .

. . . for the wrong he or she did to me. It has helped me more
than you can imagine. It is all about your choice. Choose
today to pray, then to forgive yourself and others.

Prayer of Forgiveness:

*"Heavenly Father, I choose, of my own free will, to
forgive* _____(name of person)
for (list what they did that hurt you) . . .

_____

_____

_____

. . . *I cancel all his/her debts and obligations to me and ask
You to forgive me for holding on to my unforgiveness. I come
out of agreement with my condemnations I have held. Please
cleanse my heart now of all bitterness and those places with
Your unconditional love. By Your grace I release them, in the
Name of Jesus. Amen"*

Chapter 8
Families Being Healed Through our Submission to God's Lordship— Who is your Lord?

One of the most vital, intentional actions that we can do and must choose on a daily and sometimes on a moment-by-moment basis is submitting to the Lordship of Jesus. God wants to save us and our families to be forever in eternity in His presence. Your choice to submit to His Lordship will affect your generation. *Choose today whom you will serve!*

Tanya: Honey, who are we and our family? What do we do to make our family workable – not just a term but really a "family"?

James: We are a blended family. We have two sons that we have adopted. I am the stepdad to our daughters. We must seek the Lord and know His direction as we embark upon any relationship. *In the beginning, years ago, the Lord told me that I would be a healing balm to my wife and daughters.* Daily I find myself praying and seeking the wise counsel of the Holy Spirit.

Within myself, I do not have much to offer my wife and stepdaughters. Notwithstanding, and because I bring the presence of the Lord into our household, I bring a living example to my daughters of what a real daddy should be like. This role modeling to them has brought a huge change to their lives and in my relationship to both of them. We talk through things as we spend time together. It does take time—a God-inspired plan to bring healing desired by the Lord. Time? Yes, but it has been worth it all to see how these young ladies have become amazing young women.

Our sons are on their own outside of our house, but, bless God, we have a good relationship with both of them. My heart is just filled with absolute joy when they call and just want to spend time with me. There are times we just talk, walk, and do things to have fun.

Tanya: Honey, reading this has brought me to tears of joy in that I truly see God's healing taking place in our family. One of the most valuable things I got to observe before we were married—I got to see a man who dearly loves his son. I learned later your son was the infant you adopted. My heart was so delighted to see a father truly become such a loving daddy to a little boy who became an amazing young man whom my husband adopted.

> ➢ **I have never seen such a living example of not only being a true daddy who so loves his son, but a living example of how much our Heavenly Father loves us and has adopted us as His own children into the family of God through the blood of His Own Son, our Lord Jesus Christ (Ephesians 1:5).**

This proves to me how God is absolute love.

James: Then there are times that our children need direction by asking for my advice. When I get to speak into their lives, it takes me to a deeper place with the Lord. My heart is so thankful, yet humbled, as I face the reality that my words and actions can either build them up in the direction that will benefit them or tear them down . . . sending them into a path that God will certainly talk to me.

We need to delight ourselves in the Lord as declared in Psalms 37:4-5 committing our ways to Him (making Him the Lord of our life) and He will give us the desires of our heart. It is comprehending that all things are His and that He created all things for himself, which includes us (Colossians 1:16). This should comfort us knowing that we are part of His great creation plan, that we are not a mistake; rather He created us with a purpose in mind.

It is our great pleasure that we search out the great mysteries of the Lord and set our mind on those heavenly things that are above (Colossians 3:1-3). *For we are His* **masterpiece** *created in Christ Jesus for good works, which God prepared beforehand, that we should walk in them* (Ephesians 2:10). His workmanship, His masterpiece speaks to the ownership the Lord possesses of our life. The best thing that we can do is to accept this and enter into a partnership that says **yes** to the Lordship of Jesus. If we are unwilling to do this, then who is the Lord of our lives?

WHAT TO DO?

As a follower of the Lord, one of the greatest moments that I experience working out my salvation is getting alone with the Lord in a quiet place out in the mountains. This might not be possible for everyone; however, I pray that you find a place to be alone with the Lord; seek Him out and ask Him those deep  questions that you have about your life. He is not ignorant of those life issues; He is eagerly waiting for you to bring those cares to Him and cast them upon Him (1 Peter 5:7).

This is the process I use of making Him Lord; by giving Him every area of my life, by including those things that hurt me. Sometimes I think we have this expectation that God will take action, and yet we have not given Him true permission to take over such hurts because we have not made Him Lord of all areas of our life. *I know fully that I cannot be the godly husband that I am commanded to be or the husband that my wife deserves unless I am fully surrendered to the Lordship of Jesus.* Our kids would only get at best some old worldly wisdom, which is foolishness before the Lord, if I have not gone to the Lord and asked Him . . .

> ➢ **"Papa God, what am I to do in this situation"?**

He is our Father, so why not seek out His Fatherly advice for raising kids? We need to set aside our own pride and ask the Lord to help us in everything that we do. Yes, you're thinking since I've got these kids, I know how to be a father to them? Good luck with that attitude. Without knowing Him as my Father-God I could never have been nor will ever be a true father to my children.

My family deserves the best. The best thing that I could ever give them is a man that accepts the fact that *I am crucified with Christ and it is no longer I who live but it is Christ who lives in me.* When Jesus was here on earth, He continually said: *"I only do what I see my Father doing"* (John 5:19-20).

Tanya: When we were dating I remember when you told me how you had truly died to yourself and that you were crucified with Christ. That was one of the most profound signs for me to know you were a true man of God and filled with His Spirit. I knew I could trust you because I witnessed God living in and through you. I saw His cross operating in you—you chose to die to yourself—that made me become madly in love with you! I love to see you growing in His grace and maturing more into the image of Jesus' likeness. This is a testimony and glory to God.

PRAY, SURRENDER, AND WORSHIP

James: This same attitude should overflow into all areas of our life; even when I am at work, in any public arena, and with God's people. Am I lifting my hands up to the Lord in worship—a physical posture that says I surrender all? Do I pray at times in a kneeling position if it is physically possible ... submitting to the King Who occupies the throne of my life?

One of the things that I appreciate the most about my wife is when we both fully surrender to the Lord and kneel in *prayer*. At times we will lay flat on the ground in *full surrender to the Lord together*. You might want to challenge yourself for the next couple of weeks—even for a month—by practicing these things. See how you can physically posture yourselves during worship and prayer to make it more impactful. See if this enriches your relationships—but do so from your heart.

Tanya: Yes Honey, I love it when we pray together. *I love to pray and intercede for you* as my husband to succeed and for all our kids to succeed. I was praying through a book called *The Power of a Praying Parent* by Stormie Omartian. These are such powerful prayers that I took these prayers and prayed over all our kids and grandkids and spiritual kids to know the Lord; and to be healed and touched in every area of their lives.

I prayed daily from Isaiah 54:13:

"All your children shall be taught by the Lord, and great shall be the peace of your children."

I declared this word over all my children and still fully believe that I shall see it all come together on their behalf.

It is a powerful thing to pray, to surrender everything to the Lordship of Jesus Christ. We pray for you, dear reader, and for your family and your spouse if you are married, to be touched and healed in your family in every area. When you surrender everything to Him you will see the change and miracles in your life. We pray for His many blessings upon you. It is our hope that this section on healing has truly changed your life.

It is so important for us to live a life that glorifies God. One of the reasons it is has everything to do with being a true Christian. We want to see all our family members and friends—yes, all of those whom we love—to join us in eternity in His presence. One of the last things for anyone of us to see is to have one of our loved ones banished from the presence of the Lord into outer darkness because we did not share with them heaven's reward, the love of Jesus Christ. If we absolutely love one another the way that the Bible instructs us, then certainly we must with great conviction share the gospel of the good news of Salvation in Christ with everyone—

"For God so loved the world that He gave His only begotten Son that whosoever believes on Him shall not perish but have everlasting life" (John 3:16).

We pray and hope that you and your loved ones have received Jesus Christ as Lord and Savior.

Prayer:

Father, we pray in the name of Jesus that You would save and heal our readers, their marriages, their families, their hearts, and their lives. Lord, we lift them up to You and pray that You would touch them and that they would know You and have a personal relationship with You. We entrust them into Your hands, and we say thank You for the order and peace that You will bring into their families for your glory and Kingdom—in Jesus Name we pray— Amen.

Billy Graham "Sharing Your Faith 101" explains how one can "receive Christ"— a person needs to do 4 simple things:

- Admit you are a sinner.

- Ask forgiveness and be willing to turn away from your sins.

- Believe that Christ died for you on the cross.

116

- Receive Christ into your heart and life.[1]

In Romans 10:13 it says, *"Whoever calls upon the name of the Lord will be saved."*

Here is a prayer you can pray to receive Christ right now:

"Dear Lord Jesus, I know I am a sinner, and I ask for Your forgiveness. I believe you died for my sins and rose from the dead. I trust and follow You as my Lord and Savior. Guide my life and help me to do Your will. In your name, Amen."

Praise God, if you have sincerely prayed that simple prayer, the angels are rejoicing, and we're rejoicing with you, as you have made the most important decision in your life—your prayer from your heart by faith. Choose daily to follow Jesus and love Him and let His love radiate to all around you. Share your salvation and testimony with us and with your children and your family and friends. Find a gathering of believers in Jesus near you or on a website which is a Spirit-filled ministry that speaks about Jesus Christ, Father God, and the Holy Spirit of Truth. Abundant Blessings from Him to you and yours!

---

[1] Reference: https://billygraham.org/story/sharing-your-faith-101/

Silent & Listen
Have the Same Letters

Think About It!

SECTION FOUR: COMMUNICATION

But let your communication be, Yea, yea, Nay, nay: for whatsoever is more than these cometh of evil.

(Matthew 5:37 - KJV)

But the fruit of the Spirit is love
joy, peace,   longsuffering,
kindness,   goodness,
faithfullness   gentleness,
self-control   . . . .

Against such there is no law.

Galatians 5:22-23

Chapter 9
Communicating in a Way to Understand and Resolve Problems

Communication that Bears the Fruit of the Spirit

The following (we'd remind you) is a "casual-style conversation" between us, James and Tanya—so, the "flavor" is very conversational as it was pre-recorded . . . as is most of our text.

It is so powerful in how we use our words carefully; in the way we speak with each other to understand and resolve problems. We need to hear God's voice. We need to understand and hear His kind, gentle, and loving voice which bears the fruit of the Spirit as seen in Galatians 5:22-26. In the same way we can communicate to our spouse in a loving, kind, soft voice and tone.

Tanya: I love it when my husband, James, talks to me kindly and gently. It just helps me when he acts like Jesus—Jesus receives me, hears me, and listens to me. It helps me to feel secure when my hubby talks and listens to me with understanding. Isn't that simple, but profoundly Christ-like? I think so!

When James talks to me with love and peace in a joyful, gentle, and faithful way with self-control . . . well, this is huge!

Honey, what would you say on that kind of communication, what are your thoughts on the "*Fruit of the Spirit*"?

James: When I speak it's my responsibility to be intentional. I want the fruit of the Spirit to be the only thing that comes out of my mouth. It's also when you have the mindset of Christ that you understand the same Holy Spirit that dwells in me, dwells in you. When I speak to you, the Holy Spirit listens to everything. It's not the "fruit of the Spirit" when He hears me speak to you poorly (He does not plug His ears and doesn't hear that).

➤ **If I am speaking poorly to you, I'm actually speaking poorly to the Holy Spirit Who lives within you.**

I'm not respecting the very nature of God Who resides in you—so I'm offending not only my own wife but I'm also offending the Lord because I'm speaking poorly to the Lord because we're one. I'm actually offending myself by showing some disrespect to myself because it is outside of our oneness we can actually be offensive to the Lord and to one another. I am choosing to allow negative or harmful words into our marital covenant—breaking our true oneness.

SPEAKING KIND WORDS

Tanya: Honey, I love how we speak kindly and nicely to each other. How we have both decided as we were writing this chapter that we would always desire to talk kindly to one another, in a nice way. Speaking to one another with wholesome, edifying words even if we are tired, hungry, or even in a rush. Lord help us always to be kind, gentle, and to talk with respect and in an honorable tone of speech with each other. Our words have power and consequence. My love, how does our speech influence us?

James: I must keep in mind that my speech is always, as much as possible, under the influence of Holy Spirit, to ". . . *be gracious, seasoned with salt, so that you may know how you ought to answer each person*" (Colossians 4:6). This instruction to "*be gracious*" includes our spouse.

One of the fruits of the Spirit is being "Kind." Being *gracious* is basically another word for being kind; so it is part of the character of the fruit of the Spirit.

When I am not kind to my spouse, I know it immediately because the temperature in the room changes; and so does her attitude. I get to reap what I have sown. This to me proves that Proverbs 15:1 is so correct. That verse says: "*A soft answer turns away wrath, but a harsh word stirs up anger.*"

So, the Bible is accurate and true, because you know that if you have been married for longer than a week or have been in a relationship for any amount of time, you will have witnessed this first hand.

Focusing on negative behavior is NOT something I recommend. Rather, it is all about learning to walk in your new nature, the fruit of the Spirit. When I read 1 Thessalonians 5:11—it says:

"Therefore encourage one another and build one another up, just as you are doing."

Speaking to others in a loud voice does not manifest the fruit of the Spirit. His speaking to others through me, especially to my wife, is done in a loving way that honors the Lord.

> **Speaking the fruit of the Spirit out of my mouth is speaking forth the Lord, because it is His method of communication.**

If you think about what our communication looks like within ourselves, and if it is outside of the Lord, then it is just the world's speech coming from us.

HONEST COMMUNICATION

But what's inside should be filtered by the Spirit of God --then when it comes out, it will be honest, loving, and compassionate ...

Tanya: I have learned to be honest and open in my communication with my husband, my children, and other people because it eliminates any ground for the enemy. To speak with love and truth about everything is akin to "walking in the Light as He is in the Light."

Keeping the "truth" inside simply hurts others. But what's inside should be filtered by the Spirit of God—then when it comes out, it will be honest, loving, and compassionate; therefore, I pray and ask God for wisdom first before I speak.

James: Another part of bearing good fruit is to have honest communication with one another.

It breaks my heart when I see Christians telling lies to one another. Unfortunately, I had to learn this the hard way in making sure everything at all times is honest. Moreover, nothing should ever be exaggerated.

When we accepted the Lord as our Savior, we began the process of putting off our old nature, the nature of sin that we were born into (Colossians 3:9). Now I'm learning to walk in my new nature, the nature of Christ Jesus. Consequently, I made the decision to read the Bible more and more. Why? Well, remember what Jesus said that He is the Word.

When I read the Bible, it really is Jesus speaking His words directly to me. The Holy Spirit makes it relevant in that moment, place, and time.

This is part of how we get to love the Lord. He gets to be real and make His love real to us in this way. This is part of bearing good fruit—when we love one another. Should we take action on this?

Absolutely! Romans 12:10 says:

"Love one another with brotherly affection; ***outdo one another*** *in showing honor."*

What an amazing verse this is. We are instructed to love above and beyond in a way that honors each other. Personally, I really like this standard. The world's standard for the most part is doing just enough to make the other person happy, or until we feel that we did what our duty required us to do so we feel better about ourselves.

If all of our affection is to be honoring, then it seems to me like our speech should sound honoring as well. I would think it would be almost impossible to treat someone with honor and yet our speech is not honoring? Our speech—our fruit bearing speech—is best when we follow what Colossians 3:8 says:

"But now you must put them all away; anger, wrath, malice, slander, and obscene talk from your mouth."

Tanya: "The Power of Your Words" weekly video shared an article by Jimmy Evans. In the video he mentioned that a woman needs to talk to connect and feel nourished and secure.

Words are important, especially words between a husband and wife. Everything we say impacts those around us. It changes relationships—between us and our spouse, between us and our children, and certainly between us and God.

We need to identify the dysfunctional aspects of our communication (like speaking harshly to each other with dishonesty, silence, public and private sarcasm). These coarse expressions should be removed from our speaking and replaced with the fruit of the Spirit: love, joy, peace, patience, kindness, goodness, faithfulness, gentleness, and self-control." This is what we need to remove and replace it with: the truth which is the fruit of the Spirit!

WHEN WE MISS THE MARK

James: What great news that we have the Holy Spirit Who lives within us to help us in sanctifying our speech which should bear good fruit—the fruit that the Lord desires for us. It saddens the Holy Spirit when we miss the mark by how we speak to each other (1 Thessalonians 5:19 and Ephesians 4:30).

> ➢ **We must press toward the mark, the goal to win the prize for which God has called us heavenward in Christ Jesus. Leaning into the mark of our calling is responding to the call of the Holy Spirit to accept His help in the sanctification process of our speech.**

When we do, then our speech honors and glorifies the Lord. We can rejoice, knowing that we are being a blessing to Him, to others, and to ourselves.

125

This is the foundation from which we build; the platform that says I want to bear the fruit of the Spirit. When we do so, then most of the other areas of our life will fall into place in a way that aligns with Kingdom living. We will have His SHALOM PEACE.

Our heart must take on the proper convictions to follow what it says in James 3:9-12. We can seek the Holy Spirit and trust Him to help us in becoming a fountain that has only fresh water flowing from it. Will you seek the Holy Spirit and ask Him to help you? I personally will testify to you that should you choose to seek Him—I pray that you do—that He will be so kind and loving in order to help you overcome by having these needful victories in your life.

Tanya: I admit I am learning and growing and praying and asking God to help me to listen and hear by paying full attention to what you, Honey, are saying to me. I am so sorry to interrupt you so many times when you speak by not letting you finish your words. I trust the Holy Spirit to help me to respect and honor you more. Please forgive me for all of the harsh words I've used to hurt you purposefully or inadvertently.

James: I choose to forgive you just as Christ forgives you.

Tanya: Thank you, my love, for always forgiving me as Christ does. Thank you for always saying that you are sorry when you act or talk in harsh ways to me. I see how God is working in both of our hearts to admit our wrong and to repent quickly, and forgive each other daily.

I like a book called *Keeping Your Love On* by Danny Silk who said that spouses should ask each other: "'What do you need?' Identify your problems and communicate the message: 'I care about your needs.'"

This is so crucial at the beginning of a respectful conversation. The "listening role" is the true servant role in a respectful conversation. The listener affirms, "Right now, this conversation is about you and your needs. **A skilled listener with a servant's heart is the deadliest weapon against**

the fear bombs that threaten connection" (Ref. Danny Silk, pages 113-118). We win when we listen well. Listen deeply to feel more loved and connected. This tool will help you resolve your communication challenges.

We see the importance in the way we speak our words and choose to say: "I love you every day. I appreciate you in all that you do for me (specifically)." Honey, I appreciate your good communication skills.

Husbands need their spouse to say: "I believe in you." That is so deep for me because I have always believed in you, Honey, in all that God has given you. We've even called our website www.believingforabetteryou.com – that's because we really do believe in each other for a better you! That was really insightful.

Husbands can say, "You captivate me; you are beautiful"—and to say so from their heart. When we think about each other we should validate each other. It is the power of our words by which we sow the seeds—seeds we plant to grow a harvest.

I noticed even with our children how essential it is to speak words of life over them and to them. I say things like: "You are smart and are doing a good job of it; I am proud of you. I really mean it!"

A few days ago, as we were driving I told my daughter: "You're going to be a good mother someday and a great wife."

This really had a positive impact upon my older daughter. She responded: "I wish I recorded that!" Yes, our words have power which affect everyone and everything around us.

Listening to Understand for Each Other's Benefit

It is powerful when we listen in order to understand each other strictly for the other person's benefit and not our own. This is huge because a lot of couples argue and become antagonistic toward one another; instead, they focus on the problem—whatever it is.

The best decision is when we discuss the issue—team up together in order to resolve whatever the issue—then the solution will be made clear. Instead of contending one against the other—we aim for the solution of the issue. We're both winners—by so doing, with His Spirit, we will defeat the enemy of our souls!

The problem is usually some form of miscommunication, misunderstanding, and false assumption either one of us retains. The solution is by listening to understand each other, then praying and asking God to help us find the resolution.

> ➢ **Our top goal in all communication should be a willingness to understanding each other.**

If we cannot practice this with the ones that we love and can see, how will we increase our listening skills with the Lord?

Tanya: Honey, one of my favorite things that we say to each other is: "Can you please help me understand you? What do you mean by this or can you repeat what you said to me, I want to make sure if I heard you correctly?"

Another thing is this: Often we assume a lot of wrong and false things. That is what gets us into so much trouble—especially, women should admit we get so emotional and respond to stuff without first making sure that what we think we heard is accurate. When we fail to make sure of it, then mistrust comes in—that is where all the issues start to potentially go down the wrong communication path.

It really is so important to listen, to understand, and if in doubt of what was said, or you think what you heard was not in the character of what your spouse would normally say, then better to verify it. Honey, what would you like to say about this?

James: You're so correct. As you know that is one of my favorite things about you—if I'm uncertain or if I'm questioning what I think I heard or I'm not clear of what you said, I will say to you—and you genuinely listen:

> ➤ **"Tanya, help me understand that?"**

What you see above is one of my favorite statements because it clarifies communications or miscommunications. It gives us the opportunity to listen more carefully to what is being said. I'm not trying to sound *clickish* about it, but rather my heart says I generally want to understand to make sure that I hear you properly because I love you and want to understand you. It is also my best attempt to diffuse anything that the enemy may try to work into creating any division in our marriage.

One of my favorite verses in the Bible is found in Philippians 2:3, which says:

"Let each of you look not only to his own interest, but also to the interest of others."

This is a clear indication that the Lord wants us to look to what is the best interest of others and to set aside some of our attitude of just functioning out of duty or what benefits us the most. This verse allows me to check the attitude of my heart. When I'm listening to my wife, do I listen with the intent of keeping her best interest in mind or am I more focused on what's important for me? It's really my "heart attitude."

One of my desires as a husband is to lead my family with their best interest in the forefront of my mind. Am I a living example to them of all what Christ should look like? Certainly, that includes how I communicate with them. I want all of our kids to develop the skill of listening in order to learn and understand, as it says in Proverbs 1:5: *"Let the wise hear and increase in learning, and the one who understands obtain guidance."*

Many of us want to have direction in our lives. That is a great and noble desire. One of the paths to that is by becoming a skilled listener to genuinely try to understand others.

Personally, I am working on the skill of thinking before I speak. What is the purpose of my words that I am thinking about releasing into the world? Are they of benefit? Do they serve a good purpose, or am I just putting words out there because I think it is necessary? Do my words contain value and life? Are these words expressing uplifting thoughts? Building up instead of tearing down?

Proverbs 16:20 says:

"Whoever gives thought to the word will discover good and blessed is he who trusts in the Lord."

If God is calling me to give thought to the Word, to ponder upon what He is saying, then I should accept the invitation to be intentional with my thoughts. The promise is that by obeying this concept of giving thought, it helps me to be released into His goodness through understanding His Word. What an amazing thought that we can practice listening to God with the purpose of understanding His will by listening to our spouse to better understand them. It is a win-win situation!

Resolving Problems in a Way that honors Christ

Forgiving and praying together is what helps to resolve conflicts in any relationship. We have both learned to go and pray with the Holy Spirit about everything first before we talk or resolve big issues, offenses, hurts in our heart, and then come and talk with each other about it in a better manner.

It is amazing because the Holy Spirit desires to show us the same thing. It is powerful to pray first, then listen to what God is saying, and then talk together. We need to meet each other in the middle to compromise by understanding and talking things out thereby helping each other break through any barriers. One might consider this to be a "divine consensus."

Tanya: As I am writing this chapter, we had an issue to work through. I came to God in prayer first. Then the Holy Spirit said with assurance: "All will be okay." God brought peace and healing inside of my heart and flowed His Life within me. His love just overflowed. I look to Him first as my source and Helper of everything I really need. He always helps and fills my cup. Once I had that assurance, then I went to you, Honey, to resolve the issue.

James: It is so important in resolving problems in a way that honors God (1 Peter 2:11-12).

One thing that we know is we are on the world's stage. People are always looking at what we do, what we say; especially, if they can find a way to mock us. What's the big deal about honoring God; about living a life that represents the integrity and moral character of Jesus?

The following verse found in Proverbs has promise attached to it; so it is important. This is one of the Lord's ways of forcing the enemy to bow to Him, because of how we live our lives.

The world preaches to climb that company ladder, and if necessary, step on the hands of others that are holding onto the rungs that are our steps. Since when are we called to put our own interests ahead of others?

Proverbs 18:21 says:

"Death and life are in the power of the tongue, and those who love it will eat its fruit."

The choice belongs to us on this topic. Releasing whatever comes out of our mouths can be either a blessing or a curse—the tongue can put a curse into action! Remember we have this kind of creative power from the very nature of God because we are created in His image.

Tanya: That is huge because one of the biggest things that we learned in the beginning of our marriage, is that . . .

> ➢ **. . . the wisdom from God does not allow any corrupt communication to come out of our mouth . . .**

We should talk about everything that's in our heart that we're struggling with. We need to examine all the red flags; all the things that bother us, the things that hurt us. It is essential we talk and communicate properly with each other about these struggles. This has a lot to do with speaking with a good tone and a right attitude in the midst of our conversations.

This is really important because we do not want to—nor should we—ever speak in a demeaning way, but in a loving and respectful way seeking greater understanding (Proverbs 13:3). I think about how the Father and Son and how their fellowship is always of one mind, one heart, and one will—just like what we studied in Philippians.

We are called to uplift each other and encourage each other. We are much more able to resolve problems when our speech honors Christ. In Ephesians 4:29 it says:

> *"Let no unwholesome word proceed from your mouth, but only such a word as is good for edification to the need of the moment, so that it will give grace to those who hear it."*

Honey, what would you add to this?

James: You are correct, my love. Just because we have a misunderstanding does not give us the right at any moment to step outside of responding in a way that honors God. We shouldn't say: "Well, sweetie, now that I disagree with you I don't have to bear the fruit of the Spirit; I don't have to listen the way the book of James 1:19 says or as found in other places of the Bible which tell us to speak slowly and listen intently.

I can't take the truth of God's Word and set it aside to try to justify a behavior that is not gentle, is not kind, is not filled with self-control because that kind of behavior which casts aside the fruit of the Spirit is not representing the very nature of God Who dwells within me.

Again, it is disrespecting the Spirit of the Lord that dwells within you as well as within me. The Lord always looks at our heart as it says in James 1:26. Over the course of my life, and perhaps for all of those who are reading this, we have had those moments when we thought:

"I wish that I could just reel those words back into my mouth—I wish I had never said that!"

Then we not only live with that regret regarding what we said, but also we then have to live with the damage that our words caused. Sometimes, our words are lightly received, acknowledged as silly, out of character type statements. Notwithstanding, they are most damaging to those whom we have hurt; folks might still treat us kindly—never admitting to us how deeply our words have hurt them. But those are the ones who push us away—and we live with the hurt, the regret in that we see how their lives are negatively impacted by our very words.

The best role model of how to honor one another is looking at Jesus. He always honored His father. His words never were vulgar or destructive. If we find ourselves feeling guilty or convicted about some of our own speech and actions, remember 1 John 1:9 says:

"But if we confess our sins to Him, He is faithful to forgive us our sins and to cleanse us from all unrighteousness."

Hallelujah! This is one of the first steps into the life that you desire. You have followed exactly the instructions of 2 Timothy 2:21 which says:

"Therefore, if anyone (which is you) *cleanses himself from what is dishonorable* (your guilt from saying bad things), *he will be a vessel for an honorable use* (God did forgive you and will not hold your sin against you), *set apart as holy* (your new forgiven identity in Jesus Christ), *useful to*

the master of the house (it is not too late, God will put you into His service), *ready for every good work* (the Lord has a great plan for your life)."

Hallelujah!

There are so many blessings by honoring the Lord in all that you do.

Tanya: As we are in the middle of writing this chapter on communication. Lance Hahn, Pastor of Bridgeway Christian Church, said:

> "Communication is the key in our marriage, we don't read each other's minds; that is why we have to talk them through with each other. It is like a computer that sends messages—incoming, sending, receiving messages. Men need significance that you matter in this world as the hero. Women need security to conquer the world."

> ➤ **A healthy marriage is the cornerstone of our society—a healthy marriage influences our society, community, and even the nation. (Pastor Lance Hahn – Bridgeway Christian Church, Roseville, CA)**

We see this in another nation—Kenya. This we observed with our Kenyan couple we're mentoring. They are reaching out into the community to bring hope to many people in their nation. You can read about this toward the end of this text about how our outreach to Kenya, by God's gracious intervention, is having a spiritual impact on behalf of our Kenyan couple as we mentor them. They in turn are reaching out into the community to bring hope to many people.

Again, at the end of this book we bring out examples through emails with each other the impact that is taking place—it is amazing!

The three reasons marriage was designed are:

1. Christian marriage and family reveal who God is—how He expresses His glory.

2. Marriage is a place to be transformed by not being selfish.
3. It is a place to meet core needs like three baskets: God, Self, and spouse.

We need the right system structure not to fail. We need community, friends, and mentors to help us. We cannot expect our spouses to meet all of our needs.

It has really touched us to see how we need that balance and harmony in our marriage. Please do not compare us to anyone. We are not perfect people. We truly need to learn and grow into the image of Jesus, for He should be the standard that we want to look to, and to act like Him.

We need the power of the Holy Spirit to flow into us so we can overflow with His love and goodness onto our spouses. We pray that your words be filled with life and truth—words that will encourage one another to bear the fruit of the Spirit!

Matthew 6:33
But seek ye first the kingdom of God, and his righteousness; and all these things shall be added unto you.

Chapter 10
Money Management & Wise Stewardship

God owns all our money. It is He Who is in control of everything. He provides for all our needs:

"Everything comes from you, and we have given you only what comes from your hand" (1 Chronicles 29:12-17).

We have that posted in our bathroom as a reminder that God is in control of all. Jesus talked about money more than any other subject because He understands us and wants us to prosper and live an abundant life—He died for us to give us *"life and more abundantly!"*

Tanya: I have learned how important it is to give some, save some, and to spend some wisely. I have also learned this very practical thing is when you give 10% to God, to the Church or to give and sow an offering into ministries, as the Lord leads you, that is where the blessing comes from—our obedience out of love to God. **It leaves no room for the enemy to accuse us.**

We pray and ask the Holy Spirit where and what He wants us to give . . . it is so important to save 10% in your savings account as well. It has such a tremendous effect on our income. It has saved us from so many emergencies. This action has kept peace in our marriage and in our lives when we determine to be good stewards of our resources by tithing, giving an offering and saving. Honey, what would you say on this matter?

James: To me, it becomes a question of the heart and who is your Lord. If Jesus is truly your Lord—and you want to live a life that aligns itself with God's Word—then it's important to understand it's not a duty to tithe, it's not a duty to save—it's understanding out of our loving relationship with the Father that He wants to bless us.

When we are obedient, the blessing comes out of obedience . . . it is understanding I am a steward. We are stewards of His money. When we choose wisely in our decisions, and they align with the word of God, that is the source from when and where the blessing comes.

We are the living proof that the Lord can take the smallest things and multiply them into exceptionally large things because as it says in 1 Chronicles 29:14 that all things are by the hand of the Lord. When we understand that, and comprehend this in God's word, that is where I believe wisdom meets understanding.

The benefit is the blessing that we were able to give to ourselves, our family, and to others! It is really the Lord, and He is our Jehovah Jireh, our Provider, from Whom blessings originate. It says it so plainly in Luke 12:15:

"Take care, and be on your guard against all covetousness, for one's life does not consist in the abundance of his possessions."

We are simply stewarding— the stuff is for His usage, not our identity or security. We are not to be greedy, but it is more blessed to give than to receive (Acts 20:35).

We are simply stewarding--the stuff is for His usage, not our identity or security

Tanya: Honey, you have been helping people put their financial house in order since 2007. Does money have a big impact on the people and marriages that you encounter?

James: Sadly, when I meet with couples most of them do not have a budget. Why?

> ➢ **Most couples need to work on their communication and learn to work as a team in their marriage, and especially in their financials.**

It hurts my heart when I meet with couples and they do not know what the other is spending money on or know how much money they spend or what they have.

It is general knowledge that bad money management all too often results in a bad marriage and can lead to divorce.

What breaks my heart are these things which can be prevented so easily. One of the most important things to do is meeting with a financial professional who will do all that they can do to understand where you are financially today; how do you want your life journey to look like; and most certainly, how do you want your later years to look like? As for me, it is not a one size fits all approach; just shove everyone into mutual funds and up their 401k contribution. Why would you just assume that will fix their financial situation?

I am a big fan of saving money that captures the gains of the market, but just as importantly, to make sure they never lose a penny when the market is in a downturn. Did you save money smartly so you do not force your social security to be taxed? Up to 85% of your social security could be taxed if you do not plan properly and have the correct plans in place.

Do you have a plan in place in case life happens and you need additional money along your journey because you lost your job or became injured? Some have said "I'll take money out of my house." Did you know if you are out of work, you do not qualify? Or if injured that temporary disability does not count as income? So, what is your plan? That is why it is so important to talk to someone like myself. I don't say these pridefully—but somebody's got to tell you!

A GOOD ROLE MODEL

Tanya: Honey, I love how you educate people about how money works. I remember when I called you for your financial advice because I could trust you as a good and godly man. That led us into dating. Now we're happily married, and can help others. Please explain how you have helped me/us and others in your meetings?

James: Most of my financial appointments seem more like a counseling session; frankly, that's how initially it ought to be. We need to learn HOW money really works. Then I teach them in a simple and understandable manner. I listen carefully to each spouse, role modeling to them what it looks like to listen respectfully to the other person with the intention of bringing a solution to the ISSUE, not getting ready to defend my position.

Most of the couples that I meet with do not dislike each other. The real issue is that nobody has ever simply sat down with them and taught them how to budget, how money works, and how to develop a sound financial plan that will solve their issues, meet their financial objectives—so that they are properly prepared for life's journey.

My best recommendation for couples in the beginning is for us to pray together before we talk about money; again, role modeling to them how to start the conversation so it is productive and honors the Lord.

I encourage them to talk about their plans while holding hands, which makes it much more difficult to disagree. I have them write down what they want to see happen in their financials separately so I can meet with them and help them find a way to join their plans together in a peaceful and accommodating way.

Once we have a couple on the same page, functioning as One in Christ Jesus, then getting to setting up a budget and detailing a comprehensive financial plan is much easier. I would encourage you to spend some time talking to the Lord in prayer alone, both spouses. Then, if needed, to repent before the Lord and ask Him to help you to have a great meeting with your spouse to talk about the Lord's money.

Then make that meeting a financial planning session—then it's much easier knowing the couples are connected as one, with one goal in mind: financial peace through unity with Christ together as one.

One of the most exciting times for me is to see over the years couples who I have helped. Now they call and just thank me. They are so glad that they have only grown their accounts and have never lost a penny. **What an honor it is to help change their financial legacy which impacts their entire family, and generations to come.**

HOW TO MANAGE GOD'S MONEY WELL

Journey to Financial Freedom by Larry Burkett explains:

"The Lord talked so much about money because He knew that money would be a struggle for many of us. Because He loves us, God gave us His roadmap for handling money. Some of the topics the Bible covers are how to earn, spend, save, get out of debt, give, invest, budget, and train children to manage money."

Tanya: Honey, can you please explain in each category how to handle money?

THIS IS HOW TO HANDLE MONEY:

James: How to earn: One of the verses that challenged me the most is 1 Timothy 5:8 which says:

"But if anyone does not provide for his relatives, and especially for the members of his household, he has denied the faith and is worse than an unbeliever."

Wow, that is some strong language. I had to remember that there is no condemnation to those of us who are in Christ Jesus (Rom. 8:1). What is the purpose of this verse? To me, it means that there is more to my life of living by faith; that the Lord has even more for me. It is a call to do my part, and then trusting Him to bless my efforts by working for others.

It is not even rational to think I have the right to demand of the Lord to bless me financially if I am not planting the seeds that the Lord has given to me. I think about a farmer. Should he believe that he has the right to demand that the orchard should produce a harvest when he has not planted and then watered the seed? *We must plant and water the seed so the Lord can bring the blessing of the harvest.*

SPENDING:

Spending seems so easy, especially when the atm at the cashier says: "Approved." Most just continue in life like everything must be okay. Well, is it okay? In my experience of over thirteen years, we need to spend a little more time asking the Lord the following: "Is this how You want me to spend Your money while being in harmony with my spouse with these other expenses?" Our expenses should be the result of what we as spouses agree upon and are in alignment with the Word of God.

It concerns me when I meet with couples, or even singles who have no money or little money saved for unexpected expenses. Typically, they are already living a lifestyle beyond their means. Their image is more important than taking responsibility to prepare for the proverbial "Rainy Day." One of the great lessons of life was taught to me by my papa. He is an avid bicyclist, he is in his 80s and still does around 100 miles per week. He always brings a complete tire repair kit with him. He said that he prays that he never gets a flat tire, but the reality is flat tires are inevitable—those unexpected incidents do happen. It is not a question of *if*, it is only a matter of *when?* Being properly prepared is when you take the responsibility to prepare for those situations.

GET OUT OF DEBT:

Romans 13:8 talks about what many other Bible verses talk about, which is to *"Owe no one anything"*—do not be a slave to debt. I know, I have met people for years who say things like: "But I can't afford to pay cash for our home" (and other similar statements). This is where I believe we need to be

142

practical. I will agree that most people will have a mortgage payment. However, where I look are those other bills, the credit card bills because you were not willing to save your money and pay cash for that ninth coat that you just could not live without. So, you charged a couple of hundred dollars for something that you really do not need and will end up costing you much more. We must again ask ourselves: "Am I really doing what the Father wants me to be doing with His money?"

What we need to be focusing on is putting additional money on those existing credit card payments, starting with the credit card that charges the highest interest rate. Why? Because that is the one with the most cost of borrowing. Once we pay that one off, then take that monthly amount that we were spending on that card and apply in addition to the amount that we are paying on to the next most expensive interest rate card. Continue this pattern and you will pay off your credit card debt. Then take the total sum of those payments and pay on your existing car payment, and you will pay it off much sooner. Whatever that money amount is, put that amount into your savings account and continue to save. You will be amazed at how much you can accomplish in around 5 years. By the time that elapses you might as well become debt free and have money in the bank!

Give: It should go without saying, but we do need to give. We will go more into that shortly, but we are to give in our tithes and offerings. We are also called to be generous. I think about the story of the sheep and the goats in Matthew 25:31-46. We need to give and give generously to the actual need. If you see that someone has bald tires on their car, it is almost winter, and you see a young lady with kids getting into her car; why not put a new set of tires on that car for her! Yes, pray for her, but sometimes that single mom needs the action of love lived out with new tires. Don't miss divine opportunities—they're everywhere!

Invest: These days require you to invest into discernment. Unfortunately, there are too many people who stick you into an investment account that loses money—they know there are better options, but this pays them the most commission. What is up with that worldly thinking? Why not put your money into an account that captures those gains of the market, but never loses money? That is wise management; being a great steward of God's money. In Matthew 25:14-30 it describes the parable of the talents. Bottom line is this: God wants and expects us to grow what He gives us.

Budget: One of my favorite parts of meeting with people is helping them to get on a budget in order to discover the blessing of knowing how they are spending God's money. This is such an important step to good stewardship—knowing where the money goes so you can adjust as needed. This action will help train your children in seeing you manage God's money.

It shows them what your priorities are, and that God's Word reigns in all areas of your life. Put into place a plan whereby if anything should go wrong, you are prepared. Statistically, you will at some point in your life become disabled or hurt—unable to work for a season. You might even have an earlier than planned death, or your spouse may be called home.

Training: The training of children to manage money by being that living example. We are called to train our children in the way that they should go (Proverbs 22:6), and a *"good man leaves an inheritance to his children"* (Proverbs 13:22).

Tanya: Honey, each time I see 8:31 on the clock, I am so thankful to God for your life. Please explain by telling your amazing story to our readers.

James: Many years ago, I ate at an Ice Cream Shop in Saratoga, California. On the wallpaper it had words with a message shaped like a wreathe.

> ➤ **It said: "831 –8 letters, 3 words, and only 1 meaning—*I Love You*, John 3:16."**

That stuck with me. Tragically on August 31st (8/31) I was in an auto accident that broke my neck, tore apart my left shoulder, and did damage to my back. That accident could have been on any other date, but why August 31; 8/31? To remind me that He loves me, and that life is fragile.

We must value life for it is most important—it is the time for the Lord to transform us and through us to defeat His enemy. You have no control when accidents happen. I could have died or become paralyzed to some extent or live by a car accident. Not only did I live, but I have made, by the grace of God, a good recovery. But if I would have died—would I have been prepared? At that time, no, I was not. I only had some money in my 401k and a small term life insurance policy. Those two things totaled around $40,000 and that was it. How could I ever think or expect that my young wife, who was not working at the time, could have taken care of herself and our two sons? That amount of money would have sent them down a path that would have broken my heart just knowing that I could have forced them into struggling financially. That is one of the main reasons that I went into the financial services profession. Making sure that people are properly prepared for the: "Oh no, I cannot believe that happened just in moments! I pray that you make sure you prepare properly—for others, for yourself.

ADVERTISEMENT: Please, schedule a complimentary financial meeting with me. Professional assistance is highly advisable. I would be more than happy to help you through this process.

Tanya: God wants us to manage His money well to bring Him all the glory and honor, and to build His Kingdom here on earth. We oversee and review our financials monthly. It is being faithful to God in small things—then He will entrust us with more. We will give an account to God about all our money and talents. (Ref. Luke 16: 10-14; Matthew 25: 14-30).

TITHES AND OFFERINGS

Tithing is a test, a biblical blessing and principle. In our tithe and offering it is Jesus Who has done the perfect work.

Jesus is our High Priest after the Order of Melchizedek (Heb. 7:1-28). Abram (Abraham) was refreshed by this One without Beginning or Ending after Abram returned from the "Battle of the Kings" (Gen. 14:1-24) with *"bread and wine"* (Gen. 14:18)—Abram in return *"Gave Melchizedek, King of Righteousness and King of Salem* (Peace) *a tithe of all"* (Gen. 14:20; Heb. 7:1-2—clearly the tithe is then and now 1/10th and should be given cheerfully unto the Lord for *"God loves a cheerful giver"*—2 Cor. 9:6-7).

Abraham is the father of all who are of faith (Rom. 4:16). Abraham refused to take any of the spoil won in the Battle of the Kings—but gave of his own sustenance to him (Melchizedek) who was an archetype of our High Priest today, the Lord Jesus. Don't try to skirt the issue here because you think that in the New Testament era such a tithe is not viable—it is because today He is our King of Righteousness, King of Peace!

Our friend explained that "Jesus proved God and God opened up heaven. Jesus performed that for us for we are not under the law for He has fulfilled the law. We give by the leading of our heart as men think, so let us give." Remember, Abram/Melchizedek was before circumcision, before the Law of Moses. **We cannot try to perform by paying tithes thereby trying to earn something from God.** We give because He first has given us to do it out of obedience and love to our King Jesus. It is about the condition of our heart that God looks at more than the amount you give Him; it is out of a loving relationship we give to Him.

We always pray and ask the Holy Spirit where and what amount we should give. He would lay it on our heart, and we would give it with joy and a cheerful heart (Malachi 3:8-12; 2 Corinthians 9:6-8). It all belongs to God. How we spend, give, and save—know this, it is all His and came from Him. He is the one giving you the strength and ability to do it all (Deuteronomy 8: 18).

Tanya: The question then in most cases is, how much should we give?

James: Give as the Lord leads. We do not believe in being religious and giving you a mandate in paying 10 percent, or else. As for us, we look at Romans 8:1 which says:

"There is therefore now no condemnation for those who are in Christ Jesus."

> ➢ **The way we chose to give is based upon what is in our heart—your heart should not condemn you!**

We are able by the grace of God to tithe 10 percent; give an offering to help others and save 10 percent of our income. Some certainly believe, and we have experienced this ourselves, that the fullest blessing comes through the obedience of giving 10 percent of our gross income.

This has taken time for us to do these things. However, it is a role model not an absolute. I have met with many people for financial reviews and mathematically they cannot give but a few dollars because they cannot afford any more. I understand. Then it becomes taking the responsibility to bring order into your budget so that you can give more unto the Lord. We discovered that God is way more impressed with the condition of our heart—our motives—than with the dollar amount we give. So, pray, and give what you can. The most important part that you can do is start somewhere, some amount and just give!

Tanya: In 1 Timothy 6:10 it is usually translated:

"For the love of money is a root of all kinds of evil."

Not money itself, but the *love* of money. Therein lies a key distinction. Money itself is neither good nor evil. Money is a tool that we use to help us and others to live here. Real riches are found in our relationship with Jesus and with each other more than money in dollars. Peace is priceless.

147

Most of us want a bigger home, but we all need shelter. Most of us want a new car, but we need transportation.

God wants to transfer wealth to the righteous, so we can do the work of God that He has assigned and called us to work on behalf of His Kingdom—working in tandem with the Holy Spirit as partners. (Proverbs 13:22). I love to work with the Holy Spirit, cooperate with Him, and do the work of my Heavenly Father. It brings me great joy to please and obey my God that I love dearly. I am here to serve Him and be interrupted in my life if He wants me to accomplish His will and plan, not my own agenda. Let the money come for *its coming* from Him in any event! Believe, receive, and declare you are expecting abundance and blessing coming your way—so that you can be blessed and be a blessing to others. We say for the best is yet to come.

Let's pray this prayer:

"Lord, thank You for giving us the financial resources that You alone can give. Help us Lord to become better stewards of all that You place in our hands. Help us to manage Your property and money responsibly so we can truly honor You and for You to be glorified. Help us to communicate with each other together in a way that honors You as we surrender all of this to You; in Jesus' name. Amen."

Prayer of a Husband & Wife

Keep us, O Lord, from pettiness. Let us be thoughtful in word and deed. Help us to put away pretense and face each other in deep trust without fear or self-pity.

Surround us in Your embrace - let us discover Your deep love You share in us--O Lord, encourage us to take time to bask in Your presence--in the fellowship of the Trinity, into which You have called us.

It is through You alone that there is true intimacy in our relationship. May You be glorified in our embrace and may we never ignore, never hurt, never take each other for granted. Engrave charity and compassion upon our hearts for You and for one another--in Jesus Name

Hebrews 13:4

Marriage is honrable in all, and the marriage bed is to be undefiled;

for fornicators and adulterers Elohim shall judge.

SECTION FIVE: INTIMACY

The husband should fulfill his wife's sexual needs, and the wife should fulfill her husband's needs.

(1 Corinthians 7:3 - CSB)

Chapter 11
The Way God Designed It To Be

Tanya: God created intimacy to be beautiful and pure in the marriage bed. God designed intimacy in a covenant marriage relationship in purity and holiness aligned with the Word of God. Intimacy is closeness, spiritual, emotional, and physical where husband and wife bond in being open and honest with each other. Intimacy starts first in the spiritual realm in our close relationship with the Lord and it overflows into our relationship with our spouse to be one. It is proven beautifully where we desire each other in the proper right way without crookedness or twisted worldly ways, but instead in a godly way which is so precious in His sight. Honey, what would you want to say about that?

James: I think what we forget is that there is beauty in holiness and holiness is being set apart. Understand that we serve God who is altogether pure; there is a great reason why God called us to sexual purity—it's because He is pure and He's a God Who created us to enjoy sexual intimacy so when we do it the way that we were created and designed, then He inhabits those experiences within His purity—that's where His blessing is realized.

Paul says you know that we can choose to do anything in that all things are permissible but not all things are of benefit. We've learned this in our own lives—that is assuredly the case. Sure, there's permission to proceed with virtually anything you so desire in the marriage bed; however, not all things are beneficial. Read 1 Corinthians 10:23. What we've learned is that as you enjoy each other with purity the way that God designed, then true satisfaction and fulfillment takes place because we honor the Lord with purity in our marriage bed.

Tanya: Intimacy begins with God first in a spiritual way, then it overflows physically with our spouse out of love. My friend, Ester, explained it this way to me:

153

"Love is to give. It is dying to self for the better of another person. Where you love and respect the person like you would do to Jesus. Intimacy is the oneness of how God wanted it to be from the beginning, not an appetite of the flesh of lust, but when your soul and heart are one in love with your spouse, then it is done in purity and holiness. It is so beautiful—I can feel the presence of God coming from heaven."

We have experienced that together in our intimacy bed.

True marital intimacy is not just physical sex. It includes the spiritual and emotional aspects. Intention and honesty are other keys. Do we want to please/honor each other as a gift to us from God?

We have shared and showed you in the first chapter of our text about how we love and treat each other by being intentional, kind, all day long with surprises as the Lord leads us daily.

Tanya: Honey, tell me your thoughts on the truth and your perception of what happens in couples.

James: One of the things that happens, and probably happens rather frequently, is this: Typically, when a husband says something dumb to his wife, the wife can choose how to respond.

If a wife responds in a way that says, I forgive you after the husband apologizes and repents, the relationship is restored, and peace is preserved. But there are times when a husband says something dumb, the husband repents, and says, "I am sorry," but then the wife fails to restore her husband.

What I find is this: If a woman chooses to hold on to unforgiveness, then she loses her emotional connection with her husband. Which typically means when she is not emotionally engaged with her husband she will not physically engage with her husband. She tends to push the husband away, engage with other activities or other people. Sometimes, it can become dangerous.

During this time the husband becomes frustrated and tries to reengage with his wife which angers her because now she perceives it as you just want sex. She now wants the emotional connection, and now he really desires the physical connection that is hormonally strong now. So, what's really missing is the question. Let us consider what would happen if she would have forgiven her husband and reengaged with him physically. It could really work to her advantage, and here is why I think that way.

When a man is intimate with his wife that is when he is most vulnerable. Typically, that is when his emotions open up, and then that is where the opportunity comes for them to reconnect. It is not just physically, but heart to heart and emotionally. They begin to experience on a deeper level, the intimacy that God really designed us to enjoy which is a heart to heart; as one in the Lord. You can connect in those deeper places where the Lord intended us to connect.

Tanya: I see how unforgiveness and abuse affects intimacy. Can you please explain that process?

James: The sad truth is this: Too many couples hold on to unforgiveness. It begins to drive a wedge between them. Then the enemy is all too happy to help that wedge drive them further apart. This is one the byproducts of unforgiveness. Because if we simply chose to forgive, as Christ instructs us, it will remove all the hurt from those memories of the past—to forgive is to forget the things of the past and all the wrongdoings connected with it. Then you have the ability in Christ Jesus to treat the person as if those things never took place.

I am not talking about a man who does something truly sinful, like abuse which is unacceptable or if he got involved with some sort of sexual sin. I am just saying if a man was maybe in a bad mood and said something that did not honor

155

God and his wife—something he realized that he had said something dumb. The man needs not to use words that are abusive, such as vulgar language or belittling language. At the same time, the husband needs to live a life where he needs to live out that which is honorable in all his speech.

If he is abusive with his words then he needs to repent, which means to stop doing what he is doing and to go in a different direction. Instead, he needs to use words that lift his wife up and wash his wife in the Word like we are instructed to do as husbands—to love our wives, as Christ loves the church. When we do that, it is what allows a wife to respond from a platform of love in response to a loving person who is demonstrating in a physical form the very nature of God and His character and his attributes

Sometimes a woman can use sex as a weapon; let me define that. Here is how it goes: Perhaps a man says something inappropriate and the wife is offended. The man goes to apologize, but the woman decides to hold on to unforgiveness. When the man does not receive the physical affection that his body naturally craves, then the man sometimes looks to other means of satisfaction. At a minimum, you have caused him to fight a battle that he should not need to be fighting.

Tanya: I like how Jimmy Evans in his article about Striking Your Spiritual and Emotional Match, explains that."

"Intimacy means inner closeness. When you say, 'I want to be intimate with my spouse,' you are talking about enjoying a relationship that is not superficial. First, you regard marriage as sacred. Marriage is not just a piece of paper. It is an act of the Spirit of God—it is a covenant. In the Bible, a covenant always required sacrifice. At the last supper, Jesus said, *'This cup is the new covenant in My blood, which is shed for you'* (Luke 22:20).

"Marriage only works as a covenant bond based on sacrifice. It has no end date. It is permanent until death. It

156

says, 'I will love you sacrificially until I die.' Second, you must validate each other's emotions. Validation says, 'Even if I don't understand, what you feel is important to me because you are important to me.' *A healthy, intimate marriage requires a husband and wife who can talk to each other and share deep emotions without fear and without paying a price for it. Both of you must be each other's safest place in the world.* For an intimate marriage, you must start with the sacred commitment of a covenant. That spiritual bond gives you a foundation for emotional validation. These are crucial to building a marriage marked by intimacy."

Honey how should we treat each other with natural affection?

James: Intimacy is when a couple chooses to treat each other all day long with natural affection the way the Lord designed it. It is a result of loving each other as Christ loves the Church—"and gave Himself for her." The byproduct that results from this love in giving each other to one another can now happen naturally.

Sexual intimacy is a result of natural affection, tenderness, and gentleness which you are expressing to each other all day long. We text and talk throughout the day. Part of that communication is you expressing the fruit of the Spirit to each other. Love is gentle, it is patient, it is kind, it is all those things, and it is also forgiving.

When you choose to do these things, then being sexually intimate is normal. It becomes easier with each other and super enjoyable because you are completely connected as one in your spirit, of course, but also in your emotions. So, there is nothing to hinder each other from fully enjoying each other the way God planned it to be. Years ago, I wanted to write a book called *"It's kind of like having sex all day long"*, which is the natural expression of the God-given affection toward each other all day. That is what sets the stage emotionally to prepare each other to normally want to make Love. We are able to thoroughly enjoy it with nothing to take away or to lessen the experience because we are as one physically as we are emotionally.

This oneness carries over to our spirit; there is nothing hindering us from feeling full affection for each other. So, we can enjoy each other—freely and fully on a "sexual plain." It has nothing to do with lusting. It is based on love. Lust has to do with craving for sexual satisfaction from someone else or an unquenchable desire that never is satisfied and always wants more. godly, sexual satisfaction, when it's not lust, in the end results in a heart condition where you desire each other from a place of godly love, because you're appreciating each other—you have purity and a blameless marriage bed.

Tanya: There are many lies that women believe about their bodies; for example, being too fat is ugly which affects their intimacy in marriage. The answer to these lies is simply to replace those negative lies, phrases, and voices with the truth which is the Word of God. Say: "*I am fearfully and wonderfully made*" Psalm 139:14. You will have victory in your intimacy bed as God created it—beautifully.

When a wife cannot forgive her husband or thinks many other thoughts while she is in the middle of making love, it affects her mood and orgasm. This is so important to let go and pray and stay focused and enjoy each other by thinking only about each other in that moment. Do not get distracted by your own thoughts thinking about other things. Replace all negativity by choosing to think positive thoughts about your husband and *be in the moment.*

There are hard seasons in life when your spouse is sick and cannot give you that intimacy that you need. We need to understand and have compassion that this season will pass and not last forever. Believe that there will be better days ahead. *Know that it does not always have to be sexual intercourse. You can hug, hold, embrace each other—these are all forms of sexual satisfaction between spouses.*

We had to walk through that as we are writing this chapter. James is recovering and overcoming cancer symptoms; consequently, it is hard for him to talk, eat, taste food, kiss, be more affectionate as he was before. We pray and trust God while believing and speaking life and youth over each other. We are praying over you, our dear reader, for the Lord to comfort and give you strength. Know that you are not alone in this journey of intimacy. We understand and have gone through many difficulties—as we all have; but we overcome with the supply of the Spirit of Christ to help and strengthen us to get through into victory: "I can do all things through Christ Who strengthens me!" (Phil. 4:13)

I CAN DO
ALL THINGS
THROUGH
CHRIST
WHO STRENGTHENS ME
PHILIPPIANS 4:13

Chapter 12
The Joy of Purity

*T*anya: Honey, I love our dating process. We would say and live out the joy of purity.

James: In the beginning we had a pure relationship with each other. I told you that you would know the joy of purity because I will choose to never make you feel bad like you are depriving me of something. I told you I'm going to choose not to kiss you or even fully hug you because I never wanted to stir up any kind of bad things within us that would cause us to potentially stumble or fall into a sexual sin. So, the reward of that is because we honored God before we were married with the result that is the blessing that was brought into our marriage. *Thank you, Jesus, for helping us and we pray it helps our readers to make a wise choice in their dating process.*

Tanya: After we got married, we started serving each other out of love and honor as unto the Lord.

James: Intimacy between a husband and wife is from a place of being selfless, it can be an opportunity where you serve and give to the other putting their needs and desires first. When you do that, your own needs are naturally met through your spouse. Many men will almost want to command their wife to be intimate with them, because after all, I work hard, and I provide for you. So out of guilt the wife tries to satisfy her husband, it is not from a heart of love. She feels now obligated to him out of guilt.

Guilt is associated with unforgiveness, which is associated with the enemy. That is not a behavior characteristic of the Kingdom. Neither is selfishness because Satan is selfish. It is all about a man choosing to align himself with the Father, his love—the husband's love—becoming more loving, just like the Father desires us to love Him more and more.

We are to pour out godly love upon our wife. We are to resemble Jesus Christ, to be imitators of Christ. I think about what it says when I am reading Ephesian 1:8. It says the Father lavishes his love upon us. Well, if I am in Christ, shouldn't I also take that same love and lavish it upon my wife? It also means to pour out His love to those around me. So, there it is, it's a starting place. Intimacy, the way God designed it to be, where it really all begins

Tanya: I pray that marriages truly find their identity in the Lord and turn to the Lord and put on His love and allow the Holy Spirit to change us by His grace.

I have learned the biggest thing really is when you want another person to change; first, you need to change yourself. Look in the mirror and say: **"Well Lord, forgive me, deal with me and what is wrong with me first before I can see my husband or wife changed—change me first Lord!"** Truly, you will begin to see the change in the other person. It really, really works. It's not a "put on"—it's for real! Amen.

In 1 Corinthians 7:3-5 it says not to give the enemy any room. We are not our own, so after we take a break for prayer, we are to come back and make love. This is so important to do that in a normal way it expresses yourself by being the way God made you—just flow with it. Not in a religious way or out of worry or fear but because of the freedom that we have in Christ Jesus.

There's freedom because our bed is clean like it says in Hebrews 13:4:

"Marriage should be honored by all, and the marriage bed kept pure, for God will judge the adulterer and all the sexually immoral."

It's vitally important we understand God's will and His purpose in that He wants us to be intimately in love with each other, very deeply in love by treating each other the right way—that is the way God has designed sex to be pure and holy and righteous. When both are believers in Christ Jesus, there's a connections of two hearts; when we are married and in a marital covenant; that is where we truly love each other and connect emotionally with all God-given affection on all levels.

When we agree, we do all that we can do to keep the peace, even if you agree to disagree. Still do not allow the enemy to have any room in your intimacy in your bed. But be honest with each other in loving each other; be genuine, talk to each other about how you feel.

Listen by understanding and hearing each other out—No, remember, *SILENCE and LISTEN are almost spelled with the same letters; again, we need both to truly communicate with each other.* That will help you to be connected more deeply as one in true intimacy with each other, which represents Christ's intimacy

Tanya: What about making the wrong decision by engaging in sexually wrong things, so tell me, Honey, what you just said about walking on the wrong path about how you die on the inside, even from the hurt of a woman.

James: Proverbs 5 teaches us that an adulterous woman or a seductive woman leads one down to a pit of death:

For the lips of the adulterous woman drip Honey, and her speech is smoother than oil; but in the end she is bitter as gall, sharp as a double-edged sword. Her feet go down to death; her steps lead straight to the grave. She

gives no thought to the way of life; her paths wander aimlessly, but she does not know it.

Whether the Lord physically takes you home and you physically die; well, that is up to the Lord. But I am fully convinced the death that He was really talking about was the death that happens on the inside of a man.

Whenever you commit sexual sin, and you realize you did something wrong, then you feel guilt, you feel ashamed of yourself in front of the Lord. Out of that guilt and shame you try to always balance the scales. What I mean by that is, if I did this wrong, then I need to do something right to balance the scales in my head.

God's true desire is just to recognize that I sinned, and that He wants to restore me. His word says in 1 John 1:9, if you sin confess before God. He not only forgives you, but He cleanses you from the guilt, shame, and condemnation of your sin—but that can only happen when "we walk in the Light as He is in the light"—then the sin is exposed . . . then we confess it . . . then the blood of Jesus cleanses us from all sin . . . and then we have koinonia or fellowship with one another again!

It says he cleanses us from all unrighteousness, which is that guilt and that shame. My hope and my desire is that as men we can begin to educate each other. That one of the ways to avoid a bad mistake followed up with many other bad decisions is to immediately repent and turn to the Lord, confess it, appropriate the blood of Jesus thereby being fully washed and again in fellowship with Him and with one another. This is really the "cycle of life" provided for every believer in Jesus.

To me, as I was telling my wife, Tanya, about the way I view it: If you go into a bar, and you have a shot of tequila, and you begin to drink it, and you're like, yep, I'm actually drinking it but I'm not finishing it. Yeah, you need to set it down. Yes, you did drink some tequila. I'm not suggesting that drinking is in and of itself a sin, but what I am saying is upon realizing that what you're doing is wrong, you now have a choice to not only sit the shot down, but you have the opportunity to walk away. You can choose not to order any more drinks. Likewise you can choose to not have any sex outside of marriage.

It is the same way with sexual sin. When you have that sexual encounter, you can in the middle of your sin realize, "I know I am not supposed to be having this kind of sex." Right then and there you can choose not to order another drink—just as you can choose not to further engage in any additional sexual contact. The benefit would be you do not walk away with the guilt and shame making bad decisions out of more guilt and shame.

Tanya: Honey, could I interject something here which really concerns me? I know that there are a lot of men and women who are single—they suffer from a *seductive spirit* but they have no idea they do . . . it's controlling them. Please explain to us, before we go on any further, the meaning of this lady in Proverbs 5—this "seductress"? Specifically, these verses:

> *"For why should you, my son, be enraptured by an immoral woman, and be embraced in the arms of a seductress? For the ways of man are before the eyes of the LORD, and He ponders all his paths. His own iniquities entrap the wicked man, and he is caught in the cords of his sin . . . and in the greatness of his folly he shall go astray"* (Proverbs 5:20-23).

James: Let's spend some special time here before we move on to the root of this seductive spirit—the "seductress." First of all, it is a *mocking-questioning spirit* whose purpose is actually to control. In 2 Corinthians 11:14 it shows us how Satan disguises himself as an *"angel of light."* In a practical sense the "seducer" is not at all aligned under the Lordship of Jesus . . . neither is he/she transformed in their mind into the

165

new nature we have in Christ Jesus. This unsubmitted part of their mind—that spirit—mocks God—is aligned with the Seducer (capitalized as in "Satan"). This was displayed in the "Temptation of Jesus" by Satan in the wilderness. Satan's purpose—his intention still operates today—is to seduce us into this deceptive mindset that he can offer us more than God.

This is precisely what happened in the Garden of Eden. It calls into question: *"Did God not say?"* (Gen. 3:1-7). Satan is masquerading—Satan comes as this angel of light offering them more than what God can offer. **It's a big lie—why is God holding this back from you or keeping something more from you . . . doesn't God want you to be like Him?** The "resemblance of the Holy Spirit" is NOT the Holy Spirit. The nature of the Holy Spirit is comfort, security, wisdom, assurance, holiness, truth . . .. So, the seductive spirit—Satan—appears to look like the Holy Spirit but is faux impersonator (a false/counterfeit spirit). Deception is seduction—you are not aware of what you're getting into and/or you think what is being offered is something "you're missing out on—has God said?" This "father of lies" in whom there is no truth, no good, appears to supplement what God is leaving out (John 8:42-46).

Tanya: So I see, Honey, a lot of people, especially young people, fall into this seductive spirit because they are searching for fulfillment, love, but there is nothing but lust— they are brought into a "soul-tie" where their mind or soul is being "sucked out of them"—they have no idea what they're doing . . . so they come back to this pit again and again—even much later in life. I pray as they read this that the Holy Spirit will deliver them and set them free from this seductive spirit— in Jesus Name!

"As a dog returns to its vomit, so fools repeat their folly . . . Do you see a person wise in their own eyes? There is

more hope for a fool than for them" (Prov. 26:11-12; 2 Peter 2:22).

"If the Son will set you free, you are free indeed" (John 8:36).

Tanya: Now, I want to clarify where I originally left off that the path that you said in Proverbs chapter 5 is not dying a physical death under divine judgment; that is, as you suggest, the dying of a death inside you, because something there (the root) is not right, is beyond physical death.

James: I believe it is God's choice when He allows us to die physically; but I believe even like in the book of James 1: 13-15 it talks about the different levels of sin. When sin is conceived, you know it brings forth death, and it is not just the death of you physically. It is the death that takes place in your spirit, in your inner man; they begin to suffer. Then in comes the guilt and the shame; those things are of the enemy.

Tanya: We die inside with the shame and guilt. So, then we need to have healing through the work of the Holy Spirit. Normally, this is like dealing with the original sin, dealing with all the bad decisions you made from that sinful encounter; but then to be delivered from the guilt and the shame by asking God, "What am I missing? It is a bad habit . . . what to replace it with?"

So, even if it is a little sin and it seems like nothing, it really messes up the next generation, literally, it really affects everything. So this is why we pray that you all avoid all these horrible mistakes. We pray that all our brothers and sisters in the Lord who wish they've never committed such sin can find forgiveness and a renewed mind to go deeper into the Lord—to grow in His grace.

That's why James and I are writing this book—to free you from those bondages that keep you from obtaining God's best in your life. Our desire is that we all avoid these "pits" and live lives well-pleasing before the Lord and one another.

So, do not go down to the pit! Really, the only solution in all of this is to get inner healing—that's what you really need from the Lord. Recovery from everything dragging you into the pit comes from the Lord. Get your mind right with the Lord and be filled with His love, so we can return our love to Him and to each other.

Well, that is what we have learned is that when we receive love from God, then we return it back to Him. Same thing with each other when we receive love, we can give it back. Learn to receive the real love, not lust, real love from each other, then we give it back to the other, so that we constantly receive it and give it. That is what a healthy relationship should be.

You know, Jesus gave His New Commandment in the Upper Room and told us that the New Covenant given in Matthew, Mark and Luke was really a marriage contract (See: Romans 7:1-5) but in John's Gospel His New Covenant of marriage was expressed as His New Commandment:

"A New commandment I have given you: Love one another. As I have loved you, so you also must love one another. By this everyone will know that you are My disciples, if you love one another" (John 13:34-35).

You can do this! You can love one another because He first loved us and gave Himself for us. His New Commandment is energized by His Own love—it stems from the very Love of God wrought in Christ Jesus. The "I will" the children of Israel said to the Almighty at Mt. Sinai ended in failure on the part of the ancient Israelites—that was the first covenant of marriage (Heb. 8:7) but in the second covenant God said: "I WILL."

Yes, the Great Commandment Jesus said was to "love the Lord thy God and your neighbor as yourself"—how's that workin' for you? Well, we've come to what the Bible calls "the heavenly Mt. Zion" where it is *workin' for us all!* Because we are energized by His love flowing through us in that He has put His laws in us and written them on the *"fleshy tablets of our hearts"* (2 Cor. 3:3). It is with this love that the marriage bed can be preserved.

It is so important to be married before you have sex with your spouse because this kind of premarital sex destroys the pristine experience set forth in His Word:

> *"I am jealous for you with a godly jealousy, for I promised you to one husband, to present you as a pure virgin to Christ. I am afraid, however, that just as Eve was deceived by the serpent's cunning, your minds may be led astray from your simple and pure devotion to Christ"* (2 Cor. 11:2-3).

This cunning Serpent has messed so many people up because there is no trust. You just throw away the bonding. There is no bonding between each other because it is not based on God's Second Covenant of Marriage. It's so amazing—He had betrothed Israel to Himself forever—but she was unfaithful. But He found a way to bring her back. Moses' law of marriage and remarriage said she could never marry her first husband again if she lived in adultery. So, guess what happened?

> *For the woman which hath an husband is bound by the law to her husband so long as he liveth; but if the husband be dead, she is loosed from the law of her husband.*

> *So then if, while her husband liveth, she be married to another man, she shall be called an adulteress: but if her husband be dead, she is free from that law; so that she is no adulteress, though she be married to another man.*

> *Wherefore, my brethren, ye also are become dead to the law by the body of Christ; that ye should be married to*

another, even to him who is raised from the dead, that we should bring forth fruit unto God.

How could YHWH (Jehovah) ever remarry her? He had to die—and, guess what, we died as well—so now we are married to Him Who is raised from the dead, that we should bring forth fruit unto God. This is the New Covenant of Marriage! We have a NEW BEGINNING IN CHRIST!

So many people divorce today—they think they'll try it out to see if it'll work . . . what deception! Real love is when we choose to wait, to trust in the Lord, to exercise self-control with each other. Then we can trust each other so much more— there is no lust because you do not want to have this "try-it-out premarital sex" —instead you've waited to find the beauty and purity found in married intimacy and are living as the Lord has espoused us who are His as chaste virgins. Satan hates these example, these metaphors from God's Word because that Serpent is a rebel and thrives on our disobedience because it reflects his rebellious spirit—and not the Spirit of God.

Honey, I love it when we open up more to each other and tell each other what we need by being honest. I recognize and appreciate your need for sexual intimacy—God has placed that physical arousal within you which makes you feel amazing . . . and I want you to feel amazed.

Tanya: Tell me, Honey, how does it affect you, even with God, can you even focus on the Lord, right? How does it make a real man feel without lust, putting his wife's needs over his first? How does it help a man when his wife gives her husband the fulfillment of sexual intimacy?

James: Well because men do go through times when you know they feel down or discouraged, in the middle of just trying to press in and feel completely fulfilled, trying to stay in the presence of God, the man still needs and longs for that physical touch, the physical affirmation, the physical interaction. Sex to men is like a breath. Not everyone will agree, but when a man during those moments pursues his wife to be comforted physically, it's such a refreshing breath.

When his wife needs to respond to him and doesn't reject him, then it puts a much deeper sense in the man that says: Being with my wife is like being with the Lord in the sense that, wow, that's kind of like the Lord. He never rejects me in my moment of true, desperate need. If a wife rejects the husband during that time, it frustrates him. It is the sadness of rejection that he puts his head down and just becomes profoundly sad on the inside. Sometimes that sadness turns into anger, which can lead a man into rebellion, just like we do with God sometimes when we feel like he is not hearing us.

We feel shortchanged by the Lord, and then we go out and we find other things to fulfill us. Whenever a wife takes that moment to satisfy her husband physically, his heart, his mind, his emotions, and his spirit comes back to life and a proper alignment that says: I'm feeling completely loved; I'm feeling completely accepted and not rejected.

That makes a huge contribution to a man's faith to be on a solid footing, because the wife in those moments resembles the nature of God. A nature that says: I accept you; I am there for you at every moment but especially for your time of need. Even if you in the flesh do not particularly deserve it. But the selflessness of a wife setting aside her need to be satisfied, to make sure her husband is satisfied—that's amazing. Totally is symbolic of a godly love that says, this is unselfish love, a love that puts others first, a love that is fully accepting.

When a man doesn't get that, that man will walk out the front door, go to work and the first woman that talks to him and makes him feel accepted will just seem to show up out of nowhere. When his wife just rejected him, then the battle begins within the spirit of a man because he longs for that companionship, for acceptance, to feel like someone cares about him as a person. When he finds that outside of the marriage, that is what typically causes a man to physically mess up, because his emotional needs were not met at home.

Do not misunderstand, it is never a wife's obligation, it is not really her place to be responsible to be the complete source of a man's physical and emotional health. I mean let us get this straight. A man should be completely healthy and whole and emotionally sound with his heart, his mind, and in his spirit with the Lord. What I am talking about here is when a man struggles to satisfy his physical needs, he begins to look to his wife for comfort in those times of need, then this is when he is most vulnerable and weak.

In my mind a wise wife during those very tender and fragile moments will embrace her husband and satisfy his needs. Honestly, sometimes it is a hug and sometimes it is more than a hug. But during those very tender moments when a man is vulnerable, and he drops his strong man card and wants his wife to emotionally connect at that moment . . . that's when he is allowing his heart to begin to communicate openly. It is in those moments where a wise wife will embrace her husband and not reject him. That's what empowers the man to go much deeper with his wife because that reminds him of the depth of acceptance that the Lord has with the man, because God never rejects a man, even at his deepest moment of need. So, that's kind of what I got to say about that—I know, that's a big "order."

Tanya: Great! I see how it is so important for a wife to be open, honest, and to give her body to her husband and to be close and intimate, because it helps your husband to be closer to God and it brings you both into connection as the Lord has designed intimacy to be.

I have learned that it is wise and good for a wife to initiate sex too—not always just the man. It is a two-way street. Also, a man wants his wife to believe in him and affirm that he has significance, confidence, value, and as well as appreciate him with her words and actions from the heart. **He wants to be your hero.** Give him your heart—that is all that God wants. A man's deep desire is to have his most treasured possession to respect, appreciate and love him—utterly. Our physical body will change over time, which is exactly why we need to fall in love with the person He has given to us and to affirm who they are in Christ Jesus.

Tanya: Today was such an important day as my husband and I had such a deep intimate talk with each other. I just realized it is so foundational, like my husband said. It is really the foundation with the Lord that we have with each other. It is the horizon thing. It rises up like the cross with nothing else but the background of the horizon. It's so powerful because when we have intimacy it is really the deepest part of us. Yes, we are very vulnerable, and incredibly open but private with one another. It is here where my husband's protection surrounds me, makes me feel safe in his embrace. This is where I feel like we have gone into the deepest sanctuary, from the outer court, into the holy place, and ultimately into the Holiest of All. I say this reverently—the depth of this affects a woman whose orgasm is akin to this illustration of the Temple or Sanctuary. Does she need this deep satisfaction? Absolutely—and God wants us to go deep into the Holiest of All to experience Him to the fullest.

I know a lot of people do not know how to have sexual pleasures. They question "What's the right way; what's the wrong way"? I love the Holy Spirit Who teaches and guides us into all truth (John 16:13). I pray that your marriage really is led by the Spirit of God because He will talk, teach, and show you because he even showed my husband not to do a certain thing because it was not beneficial. It should always be above reproach. A woman wants to feel real love from the man, not just to use her body for "sexual exploitation"—just get done quickly. No, take time to talk, connect emotionally, kiss her, do a massage rub, tell her how you feel and think about her—it will help her become more aroused and open up to her husband. The book entitled *1001 Sex Secrets Every Man Should Know* by Chris Allen, speaks on page 426 about "Atmosphere, candles, potpourri, soft music"—well, that "Nancy" he was talking about was me . . . that's who I wanted to be!

That is how we need to live because otherwise it's fulfilling the lusts of our own flesh. What is your intent? What are the benefits behind your intentions? It is just so important that we stay in close communion with the Lord—indeed, this provides us to have communion with each other. That is why it is so important. That is why I put God first, and my husband second. He put me as his wife second because that is the real reflection of a mystery how Father God is so close with Jesus. There is nothing hidden between them, they are one and that's how marriage truly should be. There should be nothing hidden. We are one, we love each other, and there is no perversion in our marriage nor anything sexually bad or anything impure.

This is God's "love design"—people do not need to turn to porn to fulfill their lusts or taste of perverted things that betray their spouse. God designed us to fulfill our spouse. When people seek to fulfill the lusts of their own flesh it leaves them bereft of emotion—their emotions become jaded—there is no fulfillment, no real feeling of satisfaction. So many are messed up—no other way to say it.

My prayer is that my beloved God protects us and our kids from delusion and all this perversion which surrounds us. Yes, there is such a thing as a "spirit of perversion" wrought by what is known as a "Jezebel spirit" full of Baal worship which in ancient times, even today, is nothing more than "trafficking in the bodies and souls of men." I declare, in the Name of Jesus that this "Jezebel spirit" be sent to the pit of hell with all the sexual immorality connected with it! O Lord, replace that "pitiful spirit" with Your purity and truth, with Your Light and Holiness! Lord, clothe us with Your modesty that we be above reproach in declaring your triumph over the "course of this age"—over the spirit of Jezebel and her perversions of Baal worship! That is how we're supposed to fervently pray for one another.

We are God's children and live a Kingdom life. We should not be of this world but live in God's ways. We should be able to practice God's kingdom—and declare all His works to this generation! How we live—how we treat each other—how we love one another from the heart. This is how God has designed it from the beginning to be—because Christ paid the price. Yes, Adam and Eve messed it up. Since we are redeemed we have that original knowing and discernment . . . that wisdom and knowledge of truth, righteousness with holy and right living. Even more so, in these end times, as never before, we should be living very pure and holy lives—seeking the Lord and His coming as we search out our hearts. More than ever before we need to be close with God and with each other. It is so important for this awareness to be part of our life and intimacy.

God should be first, then us. We are in that holy triangle; the Lord is covering and protecting us. That is the fullness of holiness and truth in which we should live—yes, live in and by Him. Then He will guide us and show us. He will "direct our paths"—in the paths of His righteousness in everything we do and say. This is the Truth of the Gospel. *So, we thank you Lord for teaching us how Your life should be in everything we do and say, in Jesus name, Amen.*

Tanya: How does that make a man feel when he knows that he has satisfied his wife, by making her happy?

James: Let me just go ahead and state that which is the description of a healthy man. One of his greatest desires is to know that he can make his wife happy. When we get into intimacy there must be a reasonable amount of intimacy in a good, healthy marriage. But if the couple gets what I call "stuck in the mud"--then sometimes the wife can really help the husband out. What I mean by that is instead of saying no to him sexually, what if she gives him the opportunity to say: Yes, I want to enjoy you sexually.

This is with the understanding also that the wife has the commitment to say, I'm going to openly communicate with you the things that I enjoy and the things that I need to receive satisfaction. When the husband responds to that, and provides for her that kind of satisfaction and pleasure that she needs—well, then, as far as I'm concerned that is what most healthy men truly desire to satisfy, to please the wife and to make her happy. Then the man can sit back and go: "Wow, I am a real man. I can make my wife happy!"

It's that emotional feeling which a healthy husband has when he can really please his wife and make her happy. When he experiences that with her, then, it gives them more of a heart that says: "Wow, not only can I satisfy her and make her happy, but wow, this is actually fun and enjoyable for both of us." For a healthy man his proper response should be: "YES! I want to spend more time making my wife happy."

Now, when the wife gets satisfied, then her response should be: "Wow, when I gave my husband the opportunity to make me happy, to satisfy me, he responded in a way that really did satisfy me. So, why would I not give him more opportunity to sexually satisfy me?" The end result is now the couple is more connected, more enriched in their emotions, with expanded hearts allowing their spirits, if I can say so, to reconnect in the oneness that they already have by being in Christ.

Sometimes, their spirits are not connected in the sense that the things of the flesh, and of the world, cloud our perceptions. Things like their emotional health, past grief, or souls disconnected with one another because of strife keeps them from living out their Oneness through healthy sexual intimacy. So, when they reconnect in that, then they can re-engage in that oneness they have in Christ. Here is where their spirits are reconciled with their bodies. The sense that Oneness has now been enjoyed together because the emotions (of the heart) and the bodily joy obtained through intimacy have been fully submitted to one's spirit where the Spirit of the Lord dwells—all testify that we are one, we are rejoicing, we are satisfied. We can now fully enjoy each other, which gives no place to the enemy.

That's why the enemy likes to try to show up and create strife in marriage because he knows that if a couple enjoy each other intimately, when they're most emotionally vulnerable, both become one during that moment—emotionally and physically. It dispels the darkness by turning on the Light and allowing them to commune in their covenant marriage relationship.

As a couple we can fully say we have experienced a oneness which is both emotionally and physically fulfilling because we are one in Christ, through the marital covenant. So that is the blessing behind the scenes of what it takes. In a fully committed covenant marriage we fully enjoy sexual satisfaction and true intimacy as a married couple in a covenant marriage—that where experience the Oneness that we have in the Lord.

Tanya: That's awesome. Thank you, Jesus. Amen. Thank you, Honey, for explaining that. I know a woman wants a soft-hearted man.

What I try to explain to women is one of the worst mistakes they can make is not to participate in this loving forgiveness and acceptance with their husbands. This provides him the opportunity to release that soft-hearted expression which he longs to share with his wife. What are some practical ways to understand that?

James: Because without exception, the time when a man is most vulnerable and has a soft heart—the time he is most emotionally vulnerable—is right after he has had an orgasm during lovemaking. He is so gentle, so tender, because of the chemical release that takes place in his brain. All the Dopamine, all the serotonin, and all those feel good chemicals are released. He is like, the world is good. He walks on water all of a sudden; and emotionally he is super vulnerable. He becomes the man that the wife has been praying for!

The sad thing is a woman sometimes out of her own self-righteousness, will punish her husband, by denying him the intimacy he naturally desires. He gets to a place where he physiologically requires that his physical needs must get met. The release that takes place during such sexual intimacy is necessary because he has stored up so much testosterone in his body that it becomes a chemical reality that must be released. He becomes strong and potentially aggressive if this release does not happen soon. More often than not, he will resort to seeking out satisfaction or other ways, whether it is through pornography or adultery or whatever.

Most husbands know his prayers are hindered till things are right with his wife. But when he goes to make things right with his wife, the sad thing I see is the wife, more often than not, feels like the husband has a hidden agenda and doesn't want to talk to him because she knows the conversation will eventually circle back around to "Gee, Honey, all you want is sex." For the husband, the honest confession is: "No I just do not just want sex, I absolutely need sex, because as a man, we need sex out of the cry of our soul."

For the husband, to humble himself to come to his wife, to be honest, the wife needs to meet him in that place that says: "Okay, I want to stop defending my own self-righteousness, out of pride and arrogance and say, I will humble myself and meet you at the same place of humility, because we are husband and wife; one in Christ. There is not the elevated wife

178

and the lower man who has to come crawling to his wife and beg for sex. That is not being one in Christ, because in Christ, we are both equally one as one in Christ. But when a wife makes a man feel like he has to crawl to her and beg for sex, then that is spiritually harmful and spiritually incorrect. So, both husband and wife are both wrong.

The wife can make a choice to set aside her self-righteousness and humbles herself to say I will choose this verse: *"To put on love that binds us together in perfect harmony"* (Col. 3:14). This is that love which flows out of compassion and grace and mercy. I will choose to love my husband in this way, so he is fulfilled. It lifts him up out of that place of feeling desperate, so he can think straight. Then the husband, when he has been sexually released, can now think more clearly—he is open-hearted; he's tenderhearted. He will gladly reveal himself as more and more tender, soft-hearted toward his wife. We must both choose to set aside our arrogance, self-righteousness, and pride.

Tanya: Thank you, Lord. So the biggest thing I see here is to fix the relationship first with the husband and wife, and then men who naturally need sex like a breath of air. Actually, the wife withholds that refreshing breath if she doesn't give that intimacy to him. I see so many women controlling their man by withholding such intimacy, using sex as a weapon against him. Sometimes the woman controls the man by not giving that to him, or withholding it for money for other wrong motives. If you really think about it, that is reflective of the rebellion against God, because His Word tells us to put on the mind of Christ. What is the mind of Christ (1 Cor. 2:16)? Jesus says, I am humble and lowly in heart, which means He is humble, and he is not trying to defend a position (Matt. 11:29).

Why can't she meet her husband's needs? Because she has not been putting on the mind of Christ. Because when you put on the mind of Christ, you see your husband the way Christ sees him. When the husband puts on the mind of Christ, he sees his wife the way Christ wants him to see her. So, when they both have the mind of Christ, they can immediately make their choice—to choose to put on love, the love of God. Love is patient, kind, and all those other affirmations. Now, you can bear the fruit of the Spirit. **You are now able to meet each other as one because the truth is as the Bible says: you are one in Christ when you are married.**

Once the enemy is given ground in us, he cunningly deceives us through the back door. For example: "Oh well, I'll have sex with you whenever you stop doing this or that or start doing this or that. This is how we elevate ourselves. That kind of an attitude always upsets a husband. Once a wife manifests such an attitude in an attempt to get the husband to perform on her behalf, that is nothing more than an expression of arrogance and pride. This readily creates a reaction in the husband who's thinking: "Well, who are you to think that you're better than I am?" He will almost always, out of a sinful nature, battle against his flesh. Now here comes room for the enemy to act out his pride, prove his wife wrong. It eventually will devolve the marriage into a works-oriented marriage.

Instead of a heart motivated marriage having the heart of Christ, we now witness the husband basing his relationship with his wife on the basis of works in order to prove something to her that will impress her. That's not who he is because the wife tries to change the husband's identity by saying: "Do this, do that," and he will respond on the basis of duty because that's also in his nature—a distorted sense of responsibility. So now you have set up the stage for division. Now the enemy has the wife exercising self-righteousness which is pride, and the man is operating out of duty, which means he closes his heart toward his wife.

Alas! We have two different people trying to have oneness in Christ; however, they cannot function as one because the enemy has now got a good foothold in their relationship. The Scriptures are clear that such a marriage is the beginning of self-destruction, as the enemy continues to bring divisiveness in it; it's the beginning of the undoing of that marriage.

Love is the foundation of a true intimacy to last. A book called *What to Do When You Don't Know What to Do; Sex & Intimacy* by Dr. Henry Cloud and Dr. John Townsend explains it this way:

"Love: The Foundation: A healthy sex life begins with love. Love brings a couple together and allows sex to flourish. Love encompasses sex; it is larger than sex. Love can create the desire for sex, but when the momentary passion of sex is over, love remains. It continues and is present with the couple, holding them close to each other and to the Author of love himself."

Love is what keeps the intimacy and marriage strong.

Prayer

Father we pray in Jesus name that You help marriages truly find their identity in You and turn to You, Lord Jesus, and put Your love in their relationship by allowing the Holy Spirit to change us by Your grace. To be together as one fully in You as You have created us to be in Your image and likeness through the light and truth of Your Word. Teach us Your ways and help us to live out Your love each day. Help the singles to start out in purity and let it flow into their marriage in the bond of true purity and joy. Amen

Key Takeaways:

- Intimacy is closeness, spiritual, emotional, and physical by being open and honest.
- When you want another person to change, you've got to change yourself first.

- Intimacy begins with God first, then you can give that love to your spouse.
- The key to closeness is forgiveness, openness, honesty, understanding and prayer.
- Replace those negative lies, phrases, and voices with the truth which is the Word of God.

Blessed are the pure of Heart for They Shall See God

1 MATTHEW 5:8

Tips for singles

I in them and You in Me--that they may be perfectly united, so that the world may know that You sent Me and have loved them just as You have loved Me - John 17:23

Tips for Singles Preparing for a Relationship

by
Tanya Wheeler

Singlehood? Questions to ask yourself about how to be prepared for a relationship if you are a believer in Jesus.

The Beginning Stage of Knowing Your Value and Worth

If I were to talk with you as a single person, I would say: This is me talking to *the younger version of myself.* I wish you knew the value of who you really are, your personality, your heart's desires, your wants, and what you love and hate in your personal life. I wish you would *listen* to the inside of your heart, the inner person of yourself, and understood how much you are loved and cared for by God. You are not alone in your journey of single life. There is always someone with you. **The Holy Spirit is your companion**, your good friend to talk and be close to you within your daily walk. I wish you would concentrate less on finding your mate and spend more time focusing on the process of who you are becoming.

Walking Through an Inner Healing Process

Go deeper into the inner healing of your heart and allow the process of the Holy Spirit to minister to you. He wants to heal you from all your past hurts, betrayals, bad relationships, and experiences. *Forgive them all; let them go and be free.* Be yourself, who you were meant to be, who you were created to be. Take responsibility for your actions and choices and release any shame or guilt. When you look in the mirror, how do you see yourself? Beautiful, ugly, fat, skinny etc.? Who are you? Where do you draw your identity, your value, and your worth?

Loving Yourself

When you can love yourself for who you are, you can become everything God has called you to be, whether you stay single or married. *You can only love yourself when you know how much you are unconditionally first loved by God.* Only then can you offer and give your love to another human being. Self-love is loving yourself first by knowing your own heart and God's heart for you. As for myself, I enjoyed getting to know myself for a while before I dated anyone.

The Void Inside

No one can truly satisfy me or fill the void inside of me. No person can take away my *loneliness* or make me feel fully complete. It all begins with my relationship with God, then all else will flow in harmony. How do you think about yourself? How do you see yourself? Are you in harmony and peace with yourself? Are you confident enough in yourself? If you cannot honestly answer these questions, you are not ready for a healthy relationship.

> ➢ **Remember, you are, with other believers, espoused to be the Bride of Jesus Christ first. Your value is not based on having a relationship—you already have THE relationship!**

Beginning to Date

Dating Then and Now on Spotify's <u>Mamma Knows Best</u>, by Addison Rae and Sheri Nicole[2]

Many people are searching, praying, hoping, and waiting for the right mate to come along and help them. The truth, is *are you ready* for them? **Have you taken the time to prepare yourself to become the kind of person you**

---

[2]https://open.spotify.com/episode/0oBwGBLDhW6HSZhJrMprAN?si=ODfevvKXQhaa KCqojOF1vwWhat

would want to be with? Do you have a list of characteristics you would desire to see in your future spouse? Do they have shared interests? What do you want and do not want and what will you not allow? Is your heart ready to be committed to a real relationship?

Is the relationship *pure, equally yoked*? Do you have the same core values, beliefs and viewpoints about God? Does he/she love the Lord and you properly? If *yes*, then you are ready to date. Get to know the person and determine whether you see potential, keeping the end goal in mind. *Do not give in to being physical.* Work towards companionship and a healthy responsible relationship. Take your time in the dating process.

How to Recognize Red Flags

Watch out for red flags and run away from a toxic relationship. Know that you can never change another person under these initial circumstances. Am I willing to live with this issue if I were to get married to that person? Are there any signs of red flags of verbal abuse, body language, anger, reaction, unhealthy expectations? *Can I trust them?* What are they listening to? Who is their family? How do you feel being around them? Are you safe, comfortable, and free to be yourself? Or are you losing yourself and your identity in this relationship? Do you have any doubts, suspicions, or fears about him/her? **Avoid the temptation!** *Do not make excuses by attaching yourself and assuming that they equally care about you.* Ask yourself, would I want my child to be in a relationship like this?

Choosing Wisely

Ask yourself these valuable questions. What are their future goals in life? Do they have a vision, dreams? Do they like the same type of interests as you do in food, sports, etc.? The most important question is do they really know and love the Lord first and foremost? How do they treat you? Do you feel loved and cared for by them? Do you have peace about this relationship? Above all, pray first and *ask God if it is His perfect will for you* to marry that person. Remember to ask Him for His wisdom to help you choose wisely. Do not partner with an unbeliever. Remember, darkness cannot be with the light according to Ephesians 5:6-13; 2 Corinthians 6:14. Hear God's voice to *discern* what is from God and what is not and if that person is right for you.

In a Marriage Today article, Jimmy Evans explains:

"As human beings, we do not have the capacity to love. We are only able to love each other because, first, we are loved by God. So, when you are looking for a person who will love you, what you are really looking for is a person full of God. But if you think that a person without God can love you, you are deceived. You are setting yourself up for failure."

So, when we are attracted to someone, and we start wondering whether a potential marriage will succeed, we shouldn't be asking, *"Is this person going to love me? Am I going to be disappointed?" What we really should be asking is, "Has this person accepted Jesus Christ as Lord of their life? Does this person walk in a way dependent on the Spirit?"*

When you marry a person who honors Christ and honors the Holy Spirit, you are ready to be loved. When you do not, you are going to be disappointed. You'll get your heart broken. Remember to choose wisely with whom you want to spend your whole life.

Singles' Thoughts

There is a funny speech for singles from Steve Harvey (*Singles' Thoughts*) at:
https://www.facebook.com/SteveHarvey/videos/125831948 1018366/

These are some of the thoughts that I have received from *Singles' Thoughts*:

Maybe not to assume that there is a future mate? Just know, that's okay. I think there's a lot of pressure to be with someone. Single people are often egged on by their peers which can often lead to settling for someone who isn't the right person or who isn't worthy of their time.

I wish more women knew what they deserved. That they wouldn't settle for just "anything out there" just so they wouldn't be single. I wish they had the confidence and self-worth to either stay single or wait for someone equally yoked to them.

I love the apostle Paul's charge that it is better to be single. I would encourage single people to realize they are valuable without a partner and do not need someone to be whole. There is more to life than waiting for a spouse. But if they are marriage-minded, it is good to become the person you want to attract, to embody those qualities. Nevertheless, we are so lucky to have more time to devote to God if one is single. *Celebrate* that for starters!

Being single is about knowing God and knowing yourself. It is a journey that continues the rest of your life, no matter the stage or station in which you find yourself.

Good questions:

1) What is it that I want in life? Am I putting myself in a posture to receive it, instead of chasing it down?

2) What are my top 5 personal values and how do those manifest in my life? If I am open to being in a relationship, how would I want those values to manifest in someone else?

3) What am I doing right now to allow God to transform me into the man/woman He desires me to be?

4) Do I see myself as God sees me? Do I love myself as I am? Are there areas in my life in which I have the ability and desire to change to better reflect God's character?

There is so much on learning to be *content in your singleness* that there is a lack of motivation to live for Jesus at the same time. Then one gets discouraged about being "self-consumed" because he/she is not content. It's a vicious cycle.

It is unfortunate that women feel the need to look for a **"replacement"** husband quickly after divorce instead of asking God to heal them and fill their lives with blessings that may not include a man. These are all the comments I received from Hope Writers members.

Wrong Reasons

Many women marry men who are rich because they need money, or for their appearance. But the main thing is what is *inside the heart*, their personality, and who they really are. Sometimes it is not what we want, but what we *need*. God knows what is best for us, and He knows the past and the future with that person. Many people get married to use that person out of lust. Do not make excuses for little red flags; set your healthy boundaries knowing you are not going to allow anyone to control or hurt you.

My Story

In my past, I ignored the red warning flags that God was trying to use to get my attention and, yes, I have paid the price for that. I want to encourage you not to waste your time and energy by choosing to be with the wrong person. Begin right now to respect yourself for who you are in Christ. Walk in the value that God has given you.

I am thankful to be able to say that God restored me and prepared me for the right husband. When I least expected it, after growing close to the Lord, He brought us together as one. We experienced the joy of purity in our dating process. We continue to honor each other as unto the Lord. We chose to put on God's love daily as a married couple while serving others together as one. **It is worth the wait.**

When God brings you the right person at the right time, *you will know it in your heart*. Make sure the person truly opens to you before you commit to a marriage. Get to know everything about them: their past both good and bad. Is there a fraud side of them? Who are they really, at home and in public? How do they treat others around them? Do they act one way around you and differently around others? *Be extra careful who you choose.*

Look to your relationship with Jesus for fulfillment more than in having a date or a mate. First, you must be *equally yoked* by the Lord, then your souls joined together, becoming one heart, one mind, then one body in that order. I pray and hope that this truth will help you with good direction to either find the right spouse or *celebrate your singleness.*

Thank you, and Many Blessings,

Tanya Wheeler

The Testimony of Fred & Helen from Kenya

This is our testimony to the glory of King Jesus. The Bible says in Revelation 12:11:

*"They triumphed over him (the "accuser of the brethren") by the blood of the lamb and **by the word of their testimony**; they did not love their lives so much as to shrink from death."*

We are a married couple from Kenya, Africa. We have been blessed with two amazing children. As a couple we come from different tribes, backgrounds, and different childhood upbringing. Our marriage was not working—but that's when we thank Almighty God for locating for us His anointed servants: Rev. Tanya Wheeler and Rev. James Wheeler. The Scriptures say in Isaiah 61 that the Lord will anoint His servant with His Spirit to deliver good news to humble people, to heal the brokenhearted, to set the captives free, and to announce the year of the Lord's good will.

As a result of their calling and anointing, the Rev. Tanya and Rev. James have illuminated in all their sessions with us by His Spirit those Scriptures on love, identity, healing, closeness, problem solving, communication, intimacy, purity, forgiveness and finances—they took us through with power by equipping us to choose His love over all else.

Our marriage was on the verge of collapsing. The enemy had instilled fear and lies in our own marriage by dividing us along our native dialects in that we both speak different native languages. In John 8:44 the devil is described as a murderer from the beginning; not holding to the truth, for there is no truth in him. This beguiling Serpent speaks his native language, if you would, for he is a liar and the father of lies.

The enemy had instilled such a fear in both of us—to keep us away from fulfilling the destiny of our marriage in Jesus Christ.

Fred: I was taught to comply with my African tribal culture—literally held captive by it. That culture does not glorify Jesus. I was sick in my body and had frequent pain in my body with incessant headaches. There was no love left in me for my wife—I was living contrary to what the Scriptures teach. I did not view my wife as an equal partner in our marriage. Instead I . . .

[a] Viewed her as a little child since my culture sees women as children and doesn't allow them to make any decisions in the home. I listened to the bad council of my "cultural" elders who follow the traditions of men, instead of those relational truths taught in the Bible.

[b] I did not love my wife as a husband should love his wife; because of this I didn't treat my wife well as it clearly encourages husbands to do in the Bible. Yes, that I should love my wife as Christ loved the church; that I should wash her continuously with the Word of God.

After being taken through the session of love with both Rev. Tanya and Rev. James, I realized I was not affirming the Word of God—but I was bound by dead religion. I was nothing more than a dead, religious man—bound by the traditions of man. When I came to grips with this realization, I surrendered my life to Jesus with the full realization that the love of God for me could overcome all these sins and deficiencies—He chose me and to this day lavishes His love upon me and upon this realization now abiding within me. I gave my life to Jesus with the full understanding of God's love for me; that He chose me and continues to lavish His perfect love upon me!

Once I received Christ Jesus as my Savior and Lord, I now had access to the God of love; thus, the spirit of fear disappeared and was replaced by the love of God. My marriage started moving from a shaky foundation of fear to a sure foundation in Jesus Christ. In Isaiah 33:6 it says He will be the sure foundation for your times; therefore, I started seeking the face of the Lord in truth with my beloved wife, Helen, as we both sought a personal relationship with Jesus "together!"

It is through this mutual seeking together of the Lord's favor that the lies of the enemy, Satan, were exposed. The more quality time we spent in His presence, the closer my wife and I came together—by putting God's Word first it began to define our relationship with one another in a completely different way: the way of His eternal love where we began increasingly to share His love with each other.

From those initial breakthrough days, Colossians 3:14 became a Scripture that set the pace of our married life: "*. . . above all, clothe yourselves with love, **which binds us all together in perfect harmony.***"

By clothing ourselves with God's love it enabled me and my wife to open up to one another and thereby comprehend our identity in Christ—to receive healing; to have good communication (which is a great starting point in marriage); to forgive one another; to first have intimacy with God which has improved my intimacy with my wife; and to have purity in my behavior that results in good thoughts and actions that glorify King Jesus (Ref. Proverbs 23:7 – "*As a man thinks in his heart—so is he!*"

Forgiveness was one big part for us, because the enemy had exploited us in this area. First to me as a husband in my African culture, asking forgiveness from my wife was seen as an expression of weakness! This lie from the enemy was designed to destroy our marriage. **When this lie was exposed, I began to see Jesus as the best example of perfect forgiveness in that He forgave me all my sins; therefore, I humbled myself and chose to ask my wife**

for forgiveness—just as Jesus had forgiven me. It didn't stop there; I chose to forgive every person who had hurt me. This gave me a fresh start full of the supply of His abundant grace towards me.

The grace of salvation and the love of God through Jesus Christ upon Whom Helen and I have chosen to build our marriage, has enabled us to take many steps forward. We are still a work in progress. There are many areas yet to surrender to the glory of King Jesus.

Wow! The biggest miracle happened when Rev. Tanya lead me and Helen into receiving the fullness of the Holy Spirit with the gift of speaking in tongues! In 1 Corinthians 14 the Bible says he who speaks in **tongues**, speaks to God. We are true products of the labor of our spiritual parents in the Lord as they have continued believing for us every single day as a couple to the glory of Jesus Christ.

Helen: God restored my marriage and gave both Fred and me His peace. We praise Him for giving us one mind, one spirit, and even bringing us into the realization of His One Body—the Church of the Living God. I learned about putting God first, then my marriage and kids, in that order. These priorities allowed me to experience the Love of God firsthand. I now spend quality time with the Lord, and then quality time with my husband. My children, though young, enjoy seeing us together in love and harmony. In Colossians 3:12-13 it says:

*"Put on then, as God's chosen ones, holy and beloved, compassionate hearts, kindness, humility, meekness and patience, bearing with one another and if one has a complaint against another, **forgiving each other, as the Lord has forgiven you, so you also must forgive.**"*

I chose to forgive my husband and all those who had hurt me. I put on God's love—this gave me a solid foundation in Jesus to start a walk of victory in many areas of my life. Now, every day provides even better opportunities to strengthen my faith in the Living Lord. Me and my husband are truly products of His empowerment in that by choosing love we are progressively living every day for the glory of Jesus!

Rev. James and Rev. Tanya have mentored me and my husband. They've taken the burden for praying for us and with us once every week during the weeks we went through all the sessions. Through this we experienced Jesus in a personal way—seeing His working power healed my husband's physical body from pain and brought healing to our children.

My husband has been radically transformed through the power of God. Moreover, he no longer subscribes to his tribe's culture but to **Jesus' Culture—and so do I!** In Rev. James he has found a loving spiritual father who continues to mentor him in the Lord. He has grown in his faith in the Lord and now expresses pure love. Praise God, he continues to improve every single day by God's grace.

I have learned to spend time with God; indeed, the greatest miracle happened when I and my beloved husband received the Baptism of His Holy Spirit with the gift of tongues—now my husband speaks in tongues before the Lord and is built up, edified in the Lord—I am so very blessed!

In Rev. Tanya I have found a mum and a friend with whom I can share everything—it is like a daughter who can share with her mother. Rev. Tanya is a prayer warrior. She has encouraged me a lot to take more time in prayer in that the Bible says the Lord is at hand—He is coming soon; we should not be anxious about anything, but in everything by prayer and supplication with thanksgiving to let our requests be known to Him. In 1 Thessalonians 5:16-18 the Bible tells us to rejoice always, **pray continually,** and give thanks in all circumstances for this is God's will for us in Christ Jesus.

As a woman who wants to build her house by walking upright in the fear of the Lord, I have found a true mentor in

Rev. Tanya; she has shared with me the deep things of the Lord Jesus. She has poured out her heart as a mother would do to a daughter. In her and Rev. James we have true spiritual parents who taught us the truth based on the sure foundation of Jesus Christ. They have surely nourished and cherished us in the common salvation, the common faith, and the commonwealth of the Lord. My loving husband and I are surely a work in progress to the glory of Jesus Christ. Yes, we are believing for a "better you" only because of God's love which has been poured out upon us through our beloved sister and brother.

This is our testimony to the glory of Jesus! In 1 John 5:11 God's Word tells us that the one who believes in the Son of God has the testimony within him. Both of us, Helen and Fred, are truly humbled to share our testimony with all of you to the glory of King Jesus. Amen.

Chapter Summaries

What we have found is the absolute need for a unique book like ours. What sets ours apart is the following:

The major message of our book is about coming closer to the Lord. We want many to experience salvation in Christ and to know the love of Jesus Who gave His all for you. He is the solution, the answer to all things. Within our book is instruction, and our own thoughts, with experiences that we try to communicate in a listener to our conversation (or to our dialog) format. One of the purposes of why we chose this format is because it is needed—a more than frank and open exchange; moreover, we have not found other formats like ours. Also, we now have a workbook which is complimentary to this book.

It is about Jesus' love shown as an example through our practical conversational and instructional way to help marriages and divorcees find love, healing, and hope.

We wrote this book for three reasons:

1. To help those who are struggling in their marriage.
2. To help those who are contemplating marriage.
3. To help those who are wounded by divorce.

Again, we share our story and message of hope through a conversational style of communication. It is about our story, our journey of hope, redemption, and the power of the Holy Spirit Who has inspired many couples and singles through this means of ministry.

We write from our own history and what we believe Scripture teaches. It is our hope that the Holy Spirit uses our experiences and our words to transform your own marriage.

Had we known the principles in this book earlier in our own lives, we would have been spared many struggles in our own marriage relationship.

We both hope and pray that reading our book will prove to be a transformative experience for you. This is our hope to see readers be impacted and changed.

Role modeling is key with both of us. Seems like too many authors and speakers tell you what to do. Rarely do people show others what to do through example. Our book is full of examples of the *HOW TO*. We use our experience to give good tools as a starting point. No doubt, there will be those who find not much value in our book—that's okay. We are after those who are married, yet struggling with their relationship—we're help to help you work through "the issues."

Finally, the other audience that we are pursuing are those who are getting re-married.

We are marriage mentors and have globally helped impact marriages who have in turn helped marriages in their communities. We have helped singles make wise choices in relationships. And with the guidance and help of the Holy Spirit we have been able to give those awaiting marriage or have been divorced to give them hope and healing from our story.

Our content is solid, based upon Scripture with good advice. The topics that are part of the core foundational things which are designed to bring about solid relationships in would-be marriages or help to those struggling in their marriage.

We have 5 major sections to "our story" - Love, Identity, Healing, Communication and Intimacy. Also, we have added living testimonies of our mentorship experience with a couple who gave us permission to share their story. Finally, we've included Tips for Singles Preparing for a Relationship. Many people asked for that we include this essential group in our sharing. Now, here's the overview of each of the twelve major chapters included under the five major sections:

Chapter 1. First things first in any healthy marriage is understanding "What True Love Is". We make a firm statement about the love of God who should be the foundation and center of our marriages. We give our own examples within our text wherein we include our personal experiences and a picture of the circle of love: God, yourself, others.

Chapter 2. In this chapter we begin to help couples to understand the depth of our marriage and how it is different from a non-Christian marriage. We explain the significance that Christ was talking about the relationship that He has with the Father and how our marriage should be a mirror image of that in reflecting that relationship. Being one flesh together with Christ in the center. Also, we will add the figure of a triangle which has helped us keep strong in Harmony, Peace, and Love.

Chapter 3. One of our main talking points in life is how we have learned that our Identity in Christ is one of the most important issues to comprehend. When we have a clearer picture and understanding of who we are in Christ, many negative things in our life are resolved. To know who we are, our identity, and the how and why we are being conformed to the image of Christ Jesus.

Chapter 4 and 5 We've grouped these two chapters in the review because these chapters begin to bring personal clarification to who we are distinct in ourselves; how we have as male and female different roles to fulfill and how that is impacted by who we are in Christ. We discuss in detail what each role should look like, a role modeling example. As a Woman and a Man we provide detail descriptions of each and the needs of each.

Chapter 6. Admitting that we are broken and that we have incurred harm from this world is necessary for healing to begin in a relationship. Knowing that the Lord wants us to be healthy and whole as a person is mandatory in building a healthy relationship. Healing from our past is critical to move on. Each person in the relationship needs to deal with their difficult issues and to heal in order to be whole and restored.

Chapter 7. This is where the rubber meets the road. When we learn of the power of God's Word as a healing balm, it will begin to create the hunger for more of His nourishing Word in our lives. The enemy is actively at work trying to destroy these areas of our lives. We give great instruction on how to win in these areas. Allowing the Holy Spirit to minister into the depths of our being—getting at those harmful issues which isolate and divide us from one another.

Chapter 8. Knowing Who is Lord of your life is one thing; however, choosing to make Him Lord is another. This chapter will help challenge a person to see the benefits of making the Lord the ruling King in your life as He builds His Kingdom to express His glory. Also, our family legacy here is impactful.

Chapter 9. Most of us know people who communicate in a way that is toxic, or at a minimum damaging to others. We role model our communication as an example of how to speak to each other properly, and why. Understanding begins when we hear each other—this is altogether imperative!

Chapter 10. James has been in financial services for over thirteen years. It's become obvious to James (now Tanya) that couples must speak about money. Too many couples do not have any skills to make a monetary plan--so this chapter will provide a starting place for that to happen. Understanding about tithe offerings, giving, and receiving—the principles of successful financial management can make or break a relationship.

Chapter 11. Understanding what God's plan and purpose is since the beginning of humanity—to know how we ought to conduct ourselves today, and why. This chapter is about what God intended for us in our sexual life. This is an expansive and in-depth presentation. Many couples struggle with this cardinal aspect of their marriage and desperately need healing where they can be brought back to a healthy relationship.

Chapter 12. After making mistakes in our lives we both realize that doing things the way the Lord wants makes for great joy and satisfaction. You will enjoy the blessings and benefits in keeping your relationship pure. It is about the joy of purity to do it the right way is a blessing both for you and for those with whom you come in contact.

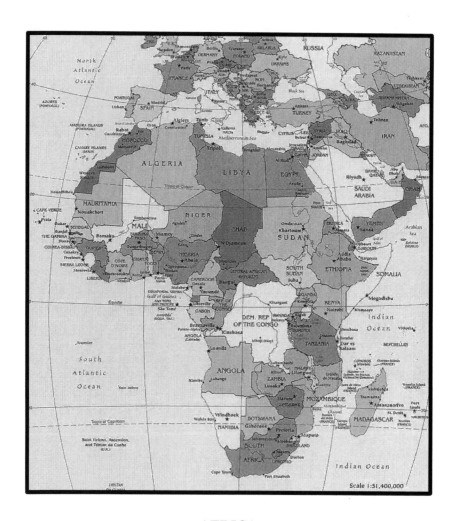

AFRICA

Epilogue – Information – Missional Needs

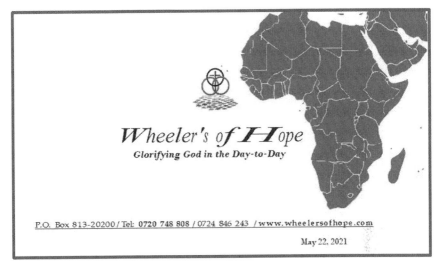

Greetings in the name of our Lord Jesus Christ:

We are so honored and humbled to write to you and truly thank God for the opportunity to share with you the vision and mission of *Wheeler's of Hope*.

We are a Jesus-centered Mission duly registered in Kenya, East Africa by the Kenyan government.

We have a God-given mandate to spread the message of salvation and hope through the transformative power of Jesus and His practical love to so many people to whom we minister—from the young to the old for the glory of God.

We answer this call by glorifying God in the day to day through putting our faith into action in serving others.

Today, we humbly request you to join us as a co-worker in this great mission of reaching the unreached and showing practical love and kindness to the needy through your prayers and financial support.

Our Vision:

Meeting the needs of the hopeless by *Wheeling them to victory* in their lives to the glory of God.

Our Mission:

Giving hope to the hopeless by raising and developing holistic individuals of integrity through their God-given abilities.

At *Wheeler's of Hope*—our Kenyan ministry—we are carrying our vision and mission through putting our faith in action to serve people we serve every single day through five distinct sub-ministries—namely:

1. **Wheeler's of Hope Education:** By helping and supporting girls and boys who are orphaned . . . many of whom come from very poor and extremely harsh backgrounds; yet they are bright. If they are given a chance to get good education and graduate they will impactfully contribute to their communities in Kenya. We are rooting for these girls and boys from such challenging backgrounds. Education provides them with security and knowledge. Help us give them Hope. In Romans 5:5 it says:

   "And hope does not put to shame, because God's love has been poured out into our hearts through the Holy Spirit, who has been given to us."

2. **Wheeler's Shelter and Daycare Center**: We have shelter which accommodates girls and women who are genuinely homeless. They are at a risk of sexual abuse in the streets. Babysitting and providing shelter for "children of the street" who so desperately need food, a place to sleep, hope and love from us as their role model parents. This

cherishing ministry helps them in nurturing a "Jesus counterculture" from a younger age. The daycare center is slowly evolving into **Wheelers Academy** which will offer primary education under a new competency-based curriculum [CBC] which is based upon the new system of education in Kenya developed by the Kenya Institute of Curriculum.

3. **Wheeler's Kitchen**: Through Wheelers Kitchen we are able to cook food and feed hundreds of street kids and street families, give them clothing, and share with them the love of God by leading them to saving faith in our Savior, the Lord Jesus Christ. Through this ministry we have seen many street children and street families open up to us about their past struggles . . . then by God's grace at work in their lives through salvation in Christ a process of healing starts. Help us reach out to more of these precious souls through the practical love of God.

4. **Wheeler's Fellowship:** We have an international fellowship which continually keeps on expanding. Where the Lord leads He both provides the wherewithal and the souls for His Kingdom! Through this ministry many marriages, entire families, and individual relationships with God and fellow human beings have been restored. Also, through this fellowship we are witnessing leaders being raised up in various Kenyan counties, who have a desire to serve the Lord.

5. **Wheeler's Leadership Training:** It is through this fellowship that Pastor Tanya and Pastor James have started leadership training that targets leaders from all the forty-seven [47] counties of Kenya—we

thank the Lord for being a vital part of this great movement God has founded here in Kenya.

Our spiritual need as a mission.

We are, by the power of His Holy Spirit, continuing to win souls to Christ through teaching them about God's redeeming love—His love is pure, perfect, and is based on the truth of the gospel. Jesus has been at the center of our teaching in that He is the only way to eternal Life and Glory. Almighty God chose us and continues to lavish us with His perfect love through His Son Jesus Christ Who is our strong foundation. Our God is ONE—our God is expressed in FELLOWSHIP—distinctly Father, Son, and Holy Spirit but eternally inseparable. We stand amazed that we have been called into the "fellowship of the Father and the Son through the Holy Spirit."

We continue to pray for more prayer partners/spiritual partners and gifted brethren who will be the next equippers and leaders for the people of Kenya.

We continue to meet and serve people with various needs both spiritual and physical. Every human being has deep spiritual needs that only the Holy Spirit can address. He alone can minister to their painful wounds of grief, guilt, resentment, reconciliation and forgiveness, self-rejection and shame. Most of the people we serve have to deal with these issues. It is here we thank the Lord for the love, care, and wisdom displayed through God's ministers, Rev. Tanya and Rev. James who faithfully have stood with us in prayer and with the practical means to carry forth the burden the Lord has placed upon our hearts.

A strong foundation for these Ministries [**Wheelers of Hope**] has been laid because we believe it is based on His unshakable foundation, Jesus Christ. In Matthew 7:24-27 it affirms to us all that the strong foundation on which we should be building has no room for fear but is undergirded by God's Holy Spirit which alone can transform us and our society to His glory. Your partnership—teaming up for the faith of the gospel (Phil. 1:27-28)—will be a glory to our Lord and a shame to our adversaries:

> *"27 Above all, you must live as citizens of heaven, conducting yourselves in a manner worthy of the Good News about Christ. Then, whether I come and see you again or only hear about you, I will know that you are standing together with one spirit and one purpose, fighting together [lit. "teaming up"] for the faith, which is the Good News. 28 Don't be intimidated in any way by your enemies. This will be a sign to them that they are going to be destroyed, but that you are going to be saved, even by God himself."* (New Living Translation)

Our financial needs as a mission

Specifically, we have financial needs in which you can participate in the areas below:

Land: We are currently occupying a facility where the lease is coming to an end by December of this year (2021). By God's grace we have identified land that is large enough to have the school, shelter, and a gathering place for praise, worship, and fellowship.

We believe with a permanently owned land for the mission, it would offer a sense of security for the children in the shelter, daycare, and the school. It would enable us to do more on the land without the concern of being ejected. The price offer on the land is **$2,600 per acre. "O Lord, do provide the 20 acres You've shown us for Your people here in Kenya!"**

Car/Van: As a mission we have a challenge of movement from one place to another with ease as we serve. We always rely on a rented car/vehicle for transport. This is quite challenging because of reliability, timeliness, and efficiency since we serve a very vast area. The need for reliable transport is so essential. With a deposit of **$5,000** we can get a van and pay the balance in installments. The total cost of the van would be **$14,000**; this is a good used van in excellent working condition. By blessing us with this vehicle we would be able to reach more people, more efficiently, to the glory of King Jesus.

Education Programs: Through our education program we have been educating girls and boys from challenging backgrounds. Through this program we have a student [Cynthia Mondon] at the Maseno University main campus; another student at the Teacher Training College [Peter Makonge]; Two girls (Elizabeth and Lilian) who have completed secondary school and will attend college in September of this year; and, finally, another girl at form/level three at Kaitui Secondary School [Debra Margaret].

It's going to cost us **$2,500** every term to keep all our students in school and to meet all their needs while at school and during their short holiday at the shelter. Our new term has begun this May and we are in the second week of the term.

Feeding Programs:

Through the Wheeler's Kitchen we are feeding the hungry who include the street children and street families, as well as the elderly who have nobody to care for them. We show them the practical love of Jesus by offering well cooked food at Wheeler's Kitchen. It normally costs us **$450-$500** to keep this program running every month. The price variation is always occasioned by food prices at the market—some months our cost comes in very low, especially when we buy food during the harvest season from farmers.

Shoe Program:

We have trained some of the beneficiaries of Wheeler's of Hope on leather work at a local rehabilitation center. We have designed and fabricated shoes which we will be making by ourselves. We will give these shoes to pupils in rural schools where most children go to school barefooted. It will cost us $5 to make each pair of shoes, the only items we need are leather and sewing machines for the leather.

Cost: Open-ended—there are many bare feet in Kenya!

Once again we are honored and humbled to write to you about these needs. We thank God for the work He has begun—may we be faithful stewards over that which He has entrusted us. We believe He is faithful to see it to completion to the glory of His Name. We kindly ask you to "team-up with us!" Together we can be co-workers in Christ by putting our faith into action. We take this opportunity, deeply from our hearts, to truly thank Rev. Tanya and Rev. James for being such solid pillars—used by the Lord every single day—to continue to strengthen the mission on the strong foundation of Jesus Christ.

Yours in Faith of the Gospel,

Pastor Fred Marienga

www.wheelersofhope.com **(Please DONATE here via PayPal)**

About the Authors & Reviews & Services

James and Tanya Wheeler are servants of the Living God. They are founders of the ***Believing for a Better You*** global ministry which locally commenced in Northern California. They are ordained ministers, marriage mentors, teachers, speakers, and authors who have helped create and develop a mission based in Kenya, Africa called "Wheeler's of Hope."

This extension of the ministry has made it possible for them to reach many through radio broadcasts, mentorship, and leadership training. These platforms enable them to disciple new leaders and further the healing (restoration) of marriage relationships in Africa. *Praise be to God, and may they continue to serve in His will!*

It is their passion to help married couples grow in faith via healing and recovery from current and past hurts by leading couples into the next steps in following Christ Jesus—Who alone can redeem and restore any and all who have been previously broken or struggling in their married or single lives.

Beyond their college education, they have learned much through life experiences. They have been taught and coached by many proven leaders for many years. Looking ahead, they plan to travel and speak where God leads to encourage others to have a deeper relationship with our Savior—*so that they may know how deeply loved, accepted, and beloved they are.* They love and care about people and their desire to see transformation take place in many lives to the glory of Christ Jesus is their ministry's calling.

"The Power of Choosing Love: How Broken Pieces Can Fit Together"—along with their workbook—are designed as a step-by-step process to recovery unto abundant blessing for couples willing to take the journey with them . . . these "ministry tools" are a compilation, given in a conversational platform that is not only "real in tone" but easily understood. Let James and Tanya share with you in the first person:

James & Tanya: We are thankful to move these words from our hearts, onto paper! Our prayer is that both our new book and companion workbook will help readers develop wholesome and healthy relationships built on the foundation of Christ by gaining a deeper understanding of God's love while learning how to have a Jesus-honoring marriage in today's society.

You may be asking yourself, "Why these publications at this time . . . aren't there sufficient ministries doing the same?" As we began the process of writing *The Power of Choosing Love* (book), the workbook was birthed making a truly interactive exchange between couples enrolled in the "course" with us, James and Tanya! We believe our experiences shared in this way will be extremely helpful to so many because our journey reflects upon most who have encountered the same challenges which we faced and continue to encounter, yet by God's grace we have overcome.

Both the book and workbook will be simultaneously released. The more relationships that can be strengthened and transformed, the better! All glory be unto God!

Again, these written efforts, as well as accompanying videos (and ultimately audio versions of the same), are designed to develop a healthy and wholesome marriage relationship while bringing healing into your lives. We appreciate the journey each one of you has taken—it is unique, no doubt—but the principles found in this marriage book and companion manual will help you move forward in taking the important steps in your life and marriage relationship—*in Christ Jesus.*

- James & Tanya

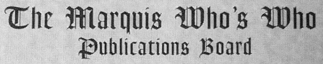

The Marquis Who's Who
Publications Board

Certifies that

James Wheeler

has hereby been approved as a subject
of biographical record in

Who's Who in America

inclusion in which is limited to individuals who possess professional integrity,
demonstrate outstanding achievement in their respective fields and have made
innumerable contributions to society as a whole.

2021-2022

Erica Lee, President

www.marquiswhoswho.com

Services

Need a Marriage Mentor?

James and I are happy you are here, and we are excited that you have decided to join us on this journey! We want you to know that if you, or someone you know, needs any additional help in marriage mentoring, you can contact us by going to the following link to schedule an appointment:

www.thepowerofchoosinglove.com -
www.believingforabetteryou.com

We provide individual and group sessions to help you in your journey of life transformation and healing. As you pray about meeting with us, remember, Jesus is the very Author and finisher of our faith; the one who has redeemed, and restored us all, and it is in Him, anything is possible!

Although we are Marriage Mentors, our services do not exclude those who are single and/or divorced. Through our ministry services and tools i.e. (books, workbooks, courses, subscriptions, audio/video, group talks), along with the individual and group mentorship services that we have available, we can help singles prepare for a marriage relationship, married couples strengthen and transform their marriage, and divorcees to take the next best steps in life. So if you fit into any of these life situations, you are in the right place!

If you are thinking about taking advantage of our mentorship services, but are undecided, and would like to see if our services are a fit for you, we are providing (for a limited time) a free thirty-minute consultation call. You can schedule your free consultation for mentorship sessions directly through our website by going to the link provided above.

Leadership Opportunity

Would you like to become a leader in your community? We will be offering a Marriage Mentor Leadership course for those who are interested in teaching these workbook sessions (with our book) within their own community and/or church.

This affordable course will help you learn the eight workbook sessions well, and lead others in your group towards a Jesus-honoring marriage. Become a pillar in your community today by contacting us via our website to let us know if you would like to be on the waitlist for this leadership course!

Websites: www.thepowerofchoosinglove.com or www.believingforabetteryou.com

Email: believingforabetteryou@gmail.com

Phone: (916) 581-1261

Financial Services

James has been a licensed financial professional for over thirteen years and has helped many families bring their financial house in order. He has a great passion to educate people on how money works. What sets James apart from others is his ability to listen to your hopes, dreams, goals—and, he is a helpful advocate!

James makes recommendations to help you set the correct plan in motion, and does not just do the status quo. So, if you want help getting your financial house in order, Wheeler's Financial is a great place to begin your journey into financial freedom.

If this is a service that you feel fits your needs, take advantage of a free consultation today, and contact James Wheeler by emailing him @ wheelersfinancial@gmail.com with the subject line (Free Consultation).

Full List of Services:

Financial Services (*financial help*)

Marriage Mentoring (*individual/group*)

Speaking (*radio / church groups / retreats / conferences / seminars*)

Books and Workbooks (*resources for individuals/groups*)

Online Subscriptions (*course materials *audio, video, and written lessons / private groups*) **Leadership Training** (*individual/group*)

Designed Packages / Training (*marriage retreats/conferences*)

*Extra resources available specifically for this workbook include:

An Online Video Workshop (*pdf of workbook + videos for each session*)

A Digital Resource Bundle (*pdf of workbook pledges + all tear outs from the workbook*)

To find out more go to: *www.thepowerofchoosinglove.com* or *www.believingforabetteryou.com*

The Companion Workbook